LOSING CONTROL?

University Seminars
Leonard Hastings Schoff Memorial Lectures

The University Seminars at Columbia University
sponsor an annual series of lectures, with the support
of the Leonard Hastings Schoff and Suzanne Levick
Schoff Memorial Fund. A member of the Columbia
faculty is invited to deliver before a general audience
three lectures on a topic of his or her choosing.
Columbia University Press publishes the lectures.

1993	*David N. Cannadine*: The Rise and Fall
	of Class in Britain, 1700–2000
1994	*Charles Larmore*: The Romantic Legacy
1995	*Saskia Sassen*: Losing Control?
	Sovereignty in an Age of Globalization

LOSING CONTROL?

SOVEREIGNTY IN AN AGE OF GLOBALIZATION

SASKIA SASSEN

Columbia
University
Press
NEW YORK

Columbia University Press

Publishers Since 1893

New York   Chichester, West Sussex

Copyright © 1996 Columbia University Press

All rights reserved

Library of Congress

Cataloging-in-Publication Data

Sassen, Saskia.

Losing control? : sovereignty in an age of globalization / Saskia Sassen.

p.   cm. — (University seminars/Leonard Hastings Schoff memorial lectures)

Includes bibliographical references and index.

ISBN 0–231–10608–4 (acid-free paper)

1. Sovereignty.   2. State, The.   3. International economic relations.

4. Capital market.   5. Emigration and immigration.

6. Information society.   I. Title.   II. Series.

JC327.S27   1996

320.1'5—dc20   96–22691

Printed in the United States of America

10 9 8 7

6 5 4

3

For Willem S. Van Elsloo

CONTENTS

Acknowledgments ix

Introduction xi

ONE **THE STATE AND THE NEW GEOGRAPHY OF POWER** 1

TWO **ON ECONOMIC CITIZENSHIP** 33

THREE **IMMIGRATION TESTS THE NEW ORDER** 63

Notes 107

Bibliography 125

Index 141

ACKNOWLEDGMENTS

I am grateful to the Leonard Hastings Schoff Memorial Fund for its support; it was an enormous pleasure and honor to deliver the public lectures named after the fund. I want to thank the University Seminars, most particularly its director, Dean Aaron Warner, and its administrative assistant, Jessie Strader, the organizers of this annual series of lectures. I also want to thank Columbia University Press, especially its publisher and director, John Moore, for support and guidance, Anne McCoy for help during the production process, and Sarah St. Onge for her excellent copyediting; working with a press that is so supportive makes a big difference. Jagdish Bhagwati, Katherine

Newman, and John Ruggie gave wonderful introductions to each of the lectures. Durval Diaz Jr. and Arturo Sanchez provided valuable research assistance. Finally, I owe a large debt to the people who came to these lectures, for their interest, engagement, good questions, and the discussions afterward.

At various stages, portions of the manuscript were read by a large number of people, who made comments and criticisms, who disagreed and agreed with me. I want to thank them all. They have made it a better book.

The public lectures that make up this book opened up for me a field of inquiry in which I am now deeply engaged. They represent the first phase of a larger project on governance and accountability in the global economy.

The growth of a global economy in conjunction with the new telecommunications and computer networks that span the world has profoundly reconfigured institutions fundamental to processes of governance and accountability in the modern state. State sovereignty, nation-based citizenship, the institutional apparatus in charge of regulating the economy, such as central banks and monetary policies—all of these institutions are being destabilized and even transformed as a result of globalization and the new technologies. What happens to processes of governance and accountability when the fundamental institutions upon which they rest and depend are thus destabilized and transformed?

In the first chapter, "The State and the New Geography of Power," I examine how the formation of a new economic system centered on cross-border flows and global telecommunications has affected two distinctive features of the modern state: sovereignty and exclusive territoriality. What are the actual territorial and nonterritorial processes through which the global economy is constituted? To a large extent, global processes materialize in national territories. This leads to a need for deregulation and the formation of regimes that facilitate the free circulation of capital, goods, information, and services. Global cities are one example of how global processes extend into national territories and national institutional arrangements. I argue that globalization under these conditions has entailed a partial denationalizing of national territory and a partial shift of some components of state sovereignty to other institutions, from supranational entities to the global capital market.

Together with sovereignty and exclusive territoriality, citizenship marks the specificity of the modern state. It may also play a role in governing the global economy. The second chapter, "On Economic Citizenship," discusses the institution of citizenship and the impact of a strengthening global economy on the continuity and formation of the rights we associate with it, particularly rights that grant the power to demand accountability from governments. Economic globalization has transformed the territoriality and sovereignty of the nation-state; it may have as great an impact on citizenship. History shows that the shape of modern citizenship owes much to the underlying conditions of society at large. As the global economy creates new conditions, the institution of citizenship may evolve yet again. The latest bundle of rights that came with the welfare state does not constitute the ultimate definition; indeed, some of those conditions may erode, as today's welfare state crises and the growing unemployment and inequality of earnings in all highly developed countries suggest. Do they signal a change in the conditions of citizens?

Once we accept the cultural and historical specificity of concepts of civil society and citizenship in Western social and political theory, we need to reckon, at least theoretically, with the impact of global forces that challenge the authority of the nation-state and civil solidarity. In such a world, what is the analytic terrain within which the social sciences need to examine the question of rights? Do we need to expand this terrain, to introduce new elements into the discourse?

In my examination of these questions, I use the notion of "economic citizenship" as a strategic research site and nexus. This notion is not part of the history and theorization of citizenship as conventionally understood. But if the specific conditions brought on by economic globalization have contributed to yet another major transformation/evolution in the institution of citizenship—and I believe they have—then we must consider the possibility that there exists a form of economic citizenship that empowers and can demand accountability from governments. The evidence supports this notion, but the so-called economic citizenship it identifies does not belong to citizens. It belongs to firms and markets—specifically, the global financial markets—and it is located not in individuals, not in citizens, but in mostly corporate global economic actors. The fact of being global gives these actors power over individual governments, and it is this particular instantiation of the notion of economic citizenship that I address in the second chapter. I use the concept as a kind of theoretical provocation, outside the accepted lineage of the concept of citizenship.

In the third and final chapter, "Immigration Tests the New Order," I look at the tension between denationalizing economic space and renationalizing political discourse in most developed countries. Immigration provides a crucial nexus in this tension. It often becomes the main and easiest target when the issue of renationalizing enters politics. But it also brings to the fore the contradictory role of the state at this time. The state itself has been transformed by its participation in the implementation of laws and regulations necessary for economic globalization and, as I discuss in chapter 3, by its participation in the implementation of human rights. Under these conditions, what does it mean to say that the state is sovereign in the control of its borders vis-à-vis people? Has not sovereignty itself been transformed? Can we continue to take it for granted, as much of the literature on the state does over and over again, that the state has exclusive authority over the entry of non-nationals? Is the character of that exclusive authority today the same as it was before the current phase of globalization and the ascendance of human rights?

Where the effort toward forming transnational economic spaces has gone the furthest and been most formalized, it has become very clear that existing frameworks for immigration policy are problematic. The coexistence of very different regimes for the circulation of capital and people is not viable. This is most evident in the legislative work necessary for the formation of the European Union. Also apparent is the beginning of a displacement of government functions onto supragovernmental or quasi-governmental institutions and forms of legitimacy. This displacement is evident in the need to create special regimes for the circulation of service workers within both the GATT and NAFTA as part of the further internationalization of trade and investment in services. The regime governing the circulation of service workers has been separated from any notion of migration, but it represents in fact a version of temporary labor migration. It is a system for labor mobility that in good part falls under the oversight of autonomous entities that are quite separate from the government. This displacement is also evident in the legitimation process. For example, the judiciary in a number of highly developed countries has made decisions invoking international covenants, notably as to the rights of immigrants, refugees, and asylum seekers, that have gone against votes in the legislature or public opinion. The invocation of international covenants to make national policy has resulted in cases where one sector of the state is in disagreement with another. Besides signaling a de facto transnationalizing of migration policy making, this also indicates the need to deconstruct "the state" in its role in the migration process. The state itself has been transformed by this combination of developments.

The existence of two different regimes for the circulation of capital and the circulation of immigrants, as well as two equally different regimes for the protection of human rights and the protection of state sovereignty, poses problems that cannot be solved by the old rules of the game. It is in this sense that immigration is a strategic site to inquire about the limits of the new order: it feeds the renationalizing of politics and the notion of the importance of sovereign control over borders, yet it is embedded in a larger dynamic of trasnationalization of economic spaces and human rights regimes.

LOSING CONTROL?

ONE

THE STATE AND THE NEW GEOGRAPHY OF POWER

Economic globalization represents a major transformation in the territorial organization of economic activity and politico-economic power. How does it reconfigure the territorial exclusivity of sovereign states, and what does this do to both sovereignty and a system of rule based on sovereign states? Has economic globalization over the last ten or fifteen years contributed to a major institutional discontinuity in the history of the modern state, the modern interstate system, and, particularly, the system of rule?

The term *sovereignty* has a long history, beginning with Aristotle, running through Bodin and Hobbes and the

American and French revolutions, and arriving today at yet another major transformation. From being the sovereignty of the ruler, it became the will of the people as contained in the nation-state, that is, popular sovereignty. It was for a long time centered in a concern with internal order, a notion that influenced international law and politics for many centuries. Sovereignty often was "an attribute of a powerful individual whose legitimacy over territory . . . rested on a purportedly direct or delegated divine or historic authority."[1] The international legal system did not necessarily register these changes as they were happening. But by the end of World War II the notion of sovereignty based on the will of the people had become established as one of the conditions of political legitimacy for a government.[2] Article 1 of the UN Charter established as one of the purposes of the UN the development of friendly relations among states "based on respect for the principles of equal rights and self-determination of peoples"; the Universal Declaration of Human Rights of 1948, Article 21 (3), provided that the will of the people shall be the basis of authority of government . . . through elections. . . ."[3] What is significant here is that this was now expressed in a fundamental international constitutive legal document. "In international law, the sovereign had finally been dethroned."[4]

The sovereignty of the modern state was constituted in mutually exclusive territories and the concentration of sovereignty in nations. There are other systems of rule, particularly those centered in supranational organizations and emergent private transnational legal regimes, and earlier forms of such supranational powers reigned on occasion over single states, as when the League of Nations gave itself the right of intervention for the purpose of protecting minority rights. Systems of rule need not be territorial, as in certain kinds of kinship-based systems; they may not be territorially fixed, as in nomadic societies; or, while territorially fixed, they need not be exclusive.[5] In the main, however, rule in the modern world flows from the absolute sovereignty of the state over its national territory.

Achieving exclusive territoriality was no easy task. It took centuries of struggle, wars, treaties made and treaties broken, to nationalize territories along mutually exclusive lines and secure the distinctive concentration of power and system of rule that is the sovereign state. Multiple systems of rule coexisted during the transition from the medieval system of rule to the modern state: there were centralizing monarchies in Western Europe, city-states in Italy, and city-leagues in Germany.[6] Even when nation-states with exclusive territoriality and sovereignty were beginning to emerge, other forms might have become effective alternatives—for example, the Italian city-states and the Hanseatic League in northern Europe—and the formation of and claims by central states were widely contested.[7] Even now, there continue to be other forms of concentration of power and other systems of rule, for instance, nonterritorial or nonexclusive systems such as the Catholic Church and the so-called Arab nation.

There have long been problems with the exclusive territoriality of the modern state. Inevitably, one thinks of Garrett Mattingly's account of the right of embassy in medieval Europe. After succeeding brilliantly at creating mutually exclusive territories, states found there was no space left for the protected conduct of diplomacy; indeed, diplomats often felt—and indeed were—threatened, as well as pelted with vegetables. Moreover, for activities not covered by specific immunities, diplomats could be tried in the courts of the host state, just like any other subject.[8] There were various intermediate forms granting specific immunities. For example, the right of embassy could often be granted without reference to a specific sovereign, allowing subject cities to negotiate directly with one another. This form of the right of embassy became increasingly problematic when the right to embassy became a matter of sovereign recognition. As Mattingly notes, having achieved absolute sovereignty, the new states found they could only communicate with each other "by tolerating within themselves little islands of alien sovereignty."[9] The doctrine of extraterritoriality was thus the answer, and its consequences are still evident today, as when a diplomat parks anywhere in the city with impunity, de jure.[10] In the long history of securing and legitimating exclusive territoriality, particularly in this century, a variety of extraterritorial regimes have accumulated. And then there is, of course, Hugo Grotius's doctrine of mare liberum, which remains with us today.[11]

It is not enough simply to posit, as is so often done, that economic globalization has brought with it declining significance for the national state. Today, the major dynamics at work in the global economy carry the capacity to undo the particular form of the intersection of sovereignty and territory embedded in the modern state and the modern state system. But does this mean that sovereignty or territoriality are less important features in the international system?

Addressing these questions requires an examination of the major aspects of economic globalization that contribute to what I think of as a new geography of power. One much-noted fact is that firms can now operate across borders with ease; indeed, for many, this is what globalization is about. But I wish to examine three other components in the new geography of power.

The first of these components concerns the actual territories where much globalization materializes in specific institutions and processes. What kind of territoriality does this represent? The second component concerns the ascendance of a new legal regime for governing cross-border economic transactions, a trend not sufficiently recognized in the social science literature. A rather peculiar passion for legality (and lawyers) drives the globalization of the corporate economy, and there has been a massive amount of legal innovation around the growth of globalization. The third component I wish to address is the growing number of economic activities taking place in electronic space. Electronic space overrides all existing territorial jurisdiction. Further, this growing virtualization of economic activity, particularly in the leading information industries such as finance and specialized corporate services, may be contributing to a crisis in control that transcends the capacities of both the state and the institutional apparatus of the economy. The speed made possible by the new technologies is creating orders of magnitude—in, for instance, the foreign currency markets—that escape the governing capacities of private and government overseers.

Adding these three components of the new geography of power to the global footlooseness of corporate capital reveals aspects of the relation between global economy and national state that the prevalent notion of a global-national duality does not adequately or usefully capture. This duality is conceived as a mutually exclusive set of terrains where the national economy or state loses what the global economy gains. Dualization has fed the proposition that the national state must decline in a globalized economy.

Territoriality in a Global Economy

To elaborate on these three components of the new geography of power, I will begin with the question of the spaces of the global economy. What is the strategic geography of globalization or, more conceptually, the particular form of territoriality that is taking shape in the global economy today?

My starting point is a set of practices and institutions: global financial markets; the ascendance of Anglo-American law firms in international business transactions; the Uruguay Round of the GATT and the formation of the World Trade Organization (WTO); the role of credit-rating agencies and other such delightful entities in international capital markets; the provisions in the GATT and NAFTA for the circulation of service workers as part of the international trade and investment in services; and immigration, particularly the cross-border circulation of low-wage workers. In my earlier research I did not think about these subjects in terms of governance and accountability; here, I seek to understand the spatial configuration and legal/regulatory regimes that specify them.

An aspect of economic globalization that has received the most attention from general and specialized commentators is the geographic dispersal of firms' factories, offices, service outlets, and markets. One of many versions of this is the global assembly line in manufacturing, perhaps most famously dramatized by the infamous case of IBM's personal computer carrying the label Made in the USA when more than 70 percent of its component parts were manufactured overseas, typically in low-wage countries.[12] Yet another version is the export-processing zone—a special tariff and taxation regime that allows firms, mostly from high-wage countries, to export semi-processed components for further processing in low-wage countries and then to reimport them back to the country of origin without tariffs on the value added through processing. There are now hundreds of such zones; the best-known instance is the Northern Industrialization Program in Mexico, the so-called *maquiladoras*. In Mexico, there are plants from many different countries, including Japanese plants making auto parts and electronic components shipped to Japanese plants in the United States. Another common example is the offshoring of clerical work. So-called clerical factories are growing rapidly in both numbers and types of locations: they can now be found in China even though workers do not necessarily know English. The clerical work that is offshored involves largely routine data entering and is, in many ways, an extension of the common practice in the highly developed countries of locating back offices in suburban areas or shipping clerical work to private households. There are several other variations of this trend toward worldwide geographic dispersal and internationalization. Indeed, national governments have reason to know this well: they are forever struggling to capture the elusive taxes of corporations operating in more than one country.

From the perspective of the national state, specifically the state in highly developed countries, offshoring creates a space economy that goes beyond the regulatory umbrella of the state. And in this regard, the significance of the state is in decline. Here we can point only to the different ways in which globalization brings about this partial denationalizing in developing and highly developed countries. In much of the developing world, it has assumed the form of free trade zones and export manufacturing zones where firms can locate production facilities without being subject to local taxes and various other regulations; such zones exist in many Latin American and Asian countries. In these cases, an actual piece of land becomes denationalized; with financial operations, the process assumes a more institutional and functional meaning.

Conceivably, the geographic dispersal of factories and offices could have gone along with a dispersal in control and profits, a democratizing, if you will, of the corporate structure. Instead, it takes place as part of highly integrated corporate structures with strong tendencies toward concentration in control and profit appropriation. Large corporations log many of these operations as "overseas sales," and it is well known that a very high share, about 40 percent, of international trade actually occurs intrafirm, and, according to some sources, the proportion is even higher than that.[13]

There are two major implications here for the question of territoriality and sovereignty in the context of a global economy. First, when there is geographic dispersal of factories, offices, and service outlets in an integrated corporate system, particularly one with centralized top-level control, there is also a growth in central functions. Put simply, the more globalized firms become, the more their central functions grow: in importance, in complexity, and in number of transactions.[14] The sometimes staggering figures involved in this worldwide dispersal demand extensive coordination and management at parent headquarters. For instance, in the early 1990s U.S. firms had more than 18,000 affiliates overseas; less known is the fact that German firms had even more, 19,000, up from 14,000 in the early 1980s or that well over 50 percent of the workforces of firms such as Ford Motors, GM, IBM, and Exxon are overseas.[15] A lot of this dispersal has been going on for a long time, and it does not proceed under a single organizational form: behind these general figures lie many types of establishments, hierarchies of control, and degrees of autonomy.[16]

The second implication in terms of territoriality and sovereignty in a global economy is that these central functions are disproportionately concentrated in the national territories of the highly developed countries. This means that an interpretation of the impact of globalization as creating a space economy that extends beyond the regulatory capacity of a single state is only half the story. It is important to clarify here that central functions involve not only top-level headquarters but also all the top-level financial, legal, accounting, managerial, executive, and planning functions necessary to run a corporate organization operating in more than one and now often several countries. These central functions partly take place at corporate headquarters, but many have become so specialized and complex that headquarters increasingly buy them from specialized firms rather than producing them in-house. This has led to the creation of what has been called the corporate services complex, that is, the network of financial, legal, accounting, advertising, and other corporate service firms that handle the difficulties of operating in more than one national legal system, national accounting system, advertising culture, etc., and do so under conditions of rapid innovations in all these fields.[17]

As a rule, firms in more routinized lines of activity, with predominantly regional or national markets, appear to be increasingly free to move or install their headquarters outside cities, while those in highly competitive and innovative lines of activity and/or with a strong world market orientation appear to benefit from being located at the heart of major international business centers, no matter how high the costs. Both types of firms need some kind of corporate services complex, and the more specialized complexes are most likely to be in cities rather than, say, suburban office parks. Thus the agglomerations of firms carrying out central functions for the management and coordination of global economic systems are disproportionately concentrated in the highly developed countries, particularly, though not exclusively, in the kinds of cities I call global cities, such as New York, Paris, and Amsterdam.[18]

Another instance today of this negotiation between a transnational process or dynamic and a national territory is that of the global financial markets. The orders of magnitude in these markets have risen sharply, as illustrated by the estimated 75 trillion U.S. dollars in turnover in the global capital market, a major component of the global economy. These transactions are partly dependent on telecommunications systems that make possible the instantaneous transmission of money and information around the globe. Much attention has gone to the new technologies' capacity for instantaneous transmission. But equally important is the extent to which the global financial markets are located in particular cities in the highly developed countries. The degrees of concentration are unexpectedly high. For instance, international bank lending by countries increased from 1.9 trillion dollars in 1980 to 6.2 trillion dollars in 1991; seven countries accounted for 65 percent of this total in both 1980 and 1991. What countries? Yes, the usual suspects: the United States, the U.K., Japan, Switzerland, France, Germany, and Luxembourg.[19]

Stock markets worldwide have become globally integrated. Besides deregulation in the 1980s in all the major European and North American markets, the late 1980s and early 1990s saw the addition of such markets as Buenos Aires, São Paulo, Bangkok, Taipei, etc. The integration of a growing number of stock markets has contributed to raise the capital that can be mobilized through them. Worldwide market value reached 13 trillion dollars in 1995. This globally integrated stock market, which makes possible the circulation of publicly listed shares around the globe in seconds, functions within a grid of very material, physical, strategic places: that is, cities belonging to national territories.

New Legal Regimes

The operation of worldwide networks of factories, offices, and service outlets and the deregulation and global integration of stock markets have involved a variety of major and minor legal innovations. Earlier, I discussed the struggle to nationalize territory and form mutually exclusive sovereign territories, in particular the question of the right of embassy, which evolved into a form of extraterritoriality through which to resolve the tension between exclusive territoriality and the need for transactions among states. The impact of economic globalization on national territory and state sovereignty could be yet another form of such extraterritoriality, only on a much larger scale. My discussion about territory in the global economy posits that much that we describe as global, including some of the most strategic functions necessary for globalization, is grounded in national territories. Is this a form of extraterritoriality that leaves the sovereignty of the state fundamentally unaltered? Or is it a development of a different sort, one that affects the sovereignty of the state and partially transforms the notions of both territoriality and sovereignty.

To address these questions, it is necessary to examine the particular forms of legal innovation that have been produced and within which much of globalization is encased and further to consider how they interact with the state or, more specifically, with the sovereignty of the state. These legal innovations and changes are often characterized as "deregulation" and taken as somewhat of a given (though not by legal scholars). In much social science, *deregulation* is another name for the declining significance of the state. But, it seems to me, these legal changes contain a more specific process, one that along with the reconfiguration of space may signal a more fundamental transformation in the matter of sovereignty, pointing to new contents and new locations for the particular systemic property that we call sovereignty. As with the discussion of territory in the global economy, my beginning point is a set of practices and minor legal forms, microhistories, that can, however, accumulate into major trends or regimes—and I am afraid are about to do so.

Firms operating transnationally need to ensure the functions traditionally exercised by the state in the national realm of the economy, such as guaranteeing property rights and contracts.[20] Yet insofar as economic globalization extends the economy—but not the sovereignty—of the nation-state beyond its boundaries, this guarantee would appear to be threatened.

In fact, globalization has been accompanied by the creation of new legal regimes and practices and the expansion and renovation of some older forms that bypass national legal systems. Globalization and governmental deregulation have not meant the absence of regulatory regimes and institutions for the governance of international economic relations. Among the most important in the private sector today are international commercial arbitration and the variety of institutions that fulfill the rating and advisory functions that have become essential for the operation of the global economy.

Over the past twenty years, international commercial arbitration has been transformed and institutionalized as the leading contractual method for the resolution of transnational commercial disputes.[21] Again, a few figures tell a quick story. There has been an enormous growth in arbitration centers. Excluding those concerned with maritime and commodity disputes—an older tradition—there were 120 centers by 1991, with another 7 established by 1993; among the more recent are those of Bahrain, Singapore, Sydney, and Vietnam. There were about a thousand arbitrators by 1990, a number that had doubled by 1992.[22] In a major study on international commercial arbitration, Yves Dezalay and Bryant Garth find that it is a delocalized and decentralized market for the administration of international commercial disputes, connected by more or less powerful institutions and individuals who are both competitive and complementary.[23] It is in this regard a far from unitary system of justice, perhaps organized, as Dezalay and Garth put it, around one great lex mercatoria, which might have been envisioned by some of the pioneering idealists of law.[24]

Another private regulatory system is represented by the debt security or bond-rating agencies that have come to play an increasingly important role in the global economy. Two agencies dominate the market in ratings, with listings of 3 trillion U.S. dollars each: Moody's Investors Service, usually referred to as Moody's, and Standard and Poor's Ratings Group, usually referred to as Standard and Poor.[25] Ten years ago Moody's and Standard and Poor had no analysts outside the United States; by 1993 they each had about a hundred in Europe, Japan, and Australia. In his study of credit-rating processes, Sinclair found that they have leverage because of their distinct gate-keeping functions for investment funds sought by corporations and governments.[26] In this regard they can be seen as a significant force in the operation and expansion of the global economy.[27] And as with business law, the U.S. agencies have expanded their influence overseas; to some extent, their growing clout can be seen as both a function and a promoter of U.S. financial orthodoxy, particularly its short-term perspective.

AMERICANIZATION

Transnational institutions and regimes raise questions about the relation between state sovereignty and the governance of global economic processes. International commercial arbitration is basically a private justice system, and credit-rating agencies are private gate-keeping systems. With other institutions, they have emerged as important governance mechanisms whose authority is not centered in the state. The current relocation of authority has transformed the capacities of governments and can be thought of as an instance of Rosenau's "governance without government."[28] This is a subject I will explore in greater detail in the next chapter. It has also spurred the formation of transnational legal regimes, which have penetrated into national fields hitherto closed.[29] In their turn, national legal fields are becoming more internationalized in some of the major developed economies. Some of the old divisions between the national and the global are becoming weaker and, to some extent, have been neutralized. The new transnational regimes could, in principle, have assumed various forms and contents; but, in fact, they are assuming a specific form, one wherein the states of the highly developed countries play a strategic geopolitical role. The hegemony of neoliberal concepts of economic relations, with its strong emphasis on markets, deregulation, and free international trade, influenced policy in the USA and the U.K. in the 1980s and now increasingly does so in continental Europe as well. This has contributed to the formation of transnational legal regimes that are centered in Western economic concepts.[30]

Dezalay and Garth note that the "international" is itself constituted largely from a competition among national approaches. There is no global law. Martin Shapiro, too, notes that there is not much of a regime of international law, either through the establishment of a single global lawgiver and enforcer or through a nation-state consensus. He also posits that if there were, it would be an international rather than a global law; in fact, it is not even certain that the concept of law itself has become universal, that is, that human relations everywhere in the world will be governed by some, though perhaps not the same, law. The globalization of law refers to a very limited, specialized set of legal phenomena, and Shapiro argues that it will almost always refer to North America and Europe and only sometimes to Japan and some other Asian countries.[31]

The international thus emerges as a site for regulatory competition among essentially national approaches, whatever the issue: environmental protection, constitutionalism, human rights.[32] From this perspective "international" or "transnational" has become in the most recent period a form of Americanization, though the process has hardly been smooth. Contestation crops up everywhere, some of it highly visible and formalized, some of it not. In some countries, especially in Europe, there is resistance to what is perceived as the Americanization of the global capital market's standards for the regulation of financial systems and standards for reporting financial information. Sinclair notes that the internationalization of ratings by the two leading U.S. agencies could be seen as another step toward global financial integration or as fulfilling an American agenda. Resentment against U.S. agencies is clearly on the rise in Europe, as became evident when Credit Suisse was downgraded in 1991 and, in early 1992, the Swiss Bank Corporation met the same fate. Conflict is also evident in the difficulty with which foreign agencies gain SEC standing as Nationally Recognized Statistical Rating Organizations in the USA. The *Financial Times*—to mention one example—has reported on private discussions in London, Paris, and Frankfurt concerning the possibility of setting up a

Europe-wide agency to compete with the major U.S.-based agencies.[33]

The most widely recognized instance of Americanization is seen, of course, in the profound influence U.S. popular culture exerts on global culture.[34] But, though less widely recognized and more difficult to specify, it has also become very clear in the legal forms ascendant in international business transactions.[35] Through the IMF and the International Bank for Reconstruction and Development (IBRD) as well as the GATT, the U.S. vision has spread to—some would say been imposed on—the developing world.[36]

The competition among national legal systems or approaches is particularly evident in business law, where the Anglo-American model of the business enterprise and competition is beginning to replace the Continental model of legal artisans and corporatist control over the profession.[37] More generally, U.S. dominance in the global economy over the last few decades has meant that the globalization of law through private corporate law-making has assumed the form of the Americanization of commercial law.[38] Certain U.S. legal practices are being diffused throughout the world—for instance, the legal device of franchising. Shapiro notes that this may not stem only from U.S. dominance but also from common law's receptivity to contract and other commercial law innovations. For example, it is widely believed in Europe that EC legal business goes to London because lawyers there are better at legal innovations to facilitate new and evolving transnational business relations. "For whatever reasons, it is now possible to argue that American business law has become a kind of global *jus commune* incorporated explicitly or implicitly into transnational contracts and beginning to be incorporated into the case law and even the statutes of many other nations."[39]

All the reasons for this Americanization are somewhat interrelated: the rationalization of arbitration know-how, the ascendance of large Anglo-American transnational legal services firms, and the emergence of a new specialty in conflict resolution.[40] The large Anglo-American law firms that dominate the international market of business law include arbitration as one of the array of services they offer. Specialists in conflict are practitioners formed from the two great groups that have dominated legal practice in the United States: corporate lawyers, known for their competence as negotiators in the creation of contracts, and trial lawyers, whose talent lies in jury trials. The growing importance in the 1980s of such transactions as mergers and acquisitions, as well as antitrust and other litigation, contributed to a new specialization: knowing how to combine judicial attacks and behind-the-scenes negotiations to reach the optimum outcome for the client. Dezalay and Garth note that under these conditions judicial recourse becomes a weapon in a struggle that will almost certainly end before trial. Notwithstanding its deep roots in the Continental tradition, especially the French and Swiss traditions, this system of private justice is becoming increasingly Americanized.

The Virtualization of Economic Activity

The third component in the new geography of power is the growing importance of electronic space. There is much to be said on this issue. Here, I can isolate one particular matter: the distinctive challenge that the virtualization of a growing number of economic activities presents not only to the existing state regulatory apparatus but also to private-sector institutions increasingly dependent on the new technologies. Taken to its extreme, this may signal a control crisis in the making, one for which we lack an analytical vocabulary.

The questions of control here have to do not with the extension of the economy beyond the territory of the state but with digitalization—that is, electronic markets—and orders of magnitude such as those that can be achieved in the financial markets, thanks to the transaction speeds made possible by the new technologies. The best example is probably the foreign currency market, which operates largely in electronic space and has achieved volumes—a trillion dollars a day—that leave the central banks incapable of exercising the influence on exchange rates they are expected to wield (though may, in fact, not always have had). The growing virtualization of economic activities raises questions of control that also go beyond the notions of non-state-centered systems of coordination prevalent in the literature on governance.

The State Reconfigured

In many ways, the state is involved in this emerging transnational governance system. But it is a state that has itself undergone transformation and participated in legitimating a new doctrine about its role in the economy. Central to this new doctrine is a growing consensus among states to further the growth and strength of the global economy. This combination of elements is illustrated by some of the aspects of the December 1994 crisis in Mexico.

Mexico's crisis was defined rather generally in international political and business circles, and in much of the press, as the result of the global financial markets' loss of confidence in the Mexican economy and the government's leadership of it. The U.S. government defined the crisis as a global economic security issue with direct impact on the U.S. economy and pushed hard to get the U.S. legislature and the governments of other highly developed countries to come to Mexico's aid. It opted for a financial "solution," an aid package that would allow the Mexican government to pay its obligations to foreign investors and thereby restore foreign (and national) investors' confidence in the

Mexican economy. This financial response was but one of several potential choices. For instance, there could conceivably have been an emphasis on promoting manufacturing growth and protecting small businesses and homeowners from the bankruptcies faced by many in Mexico under the terms of the "financial" solution. And the U.S. government could also have exhorted the Mexican government to give up on restoring confidence in the global financial market and focus instead on the production of real value added in the Mexican economy. To complicate matters further, this crisis, which was largely presented as a global economic security issue, was handled not by the secretary of state—as it would have been twenty years ago—but by the secretary of the treasury, Robert Rubin, someone who had been the so-called dean of Wall Street. There are two rather important novel elements here: first, that Treasury should handle this international crisis, and, second, that the secretary of that agency was a former top partner at Goldman, Sachs & Co. on Wall Street, one of the leading global financial firms. My aim here is not to point to even the slightest potential for corruption but rather to raise the question of what is desirable economically, and how we define problems and their best solutions.

The shift in responsibility from the State Department to Treasury signals the extent to which the state itself has been transformed by its participation in the implementation of globalization and by the pressures of globalization. Many governments now see their responsibilities as going beyond traditional foreign policy and extending to world trade, the global environment, and global economic stability.[41] This participation of the state in the international arena is an extremely multifaceted and complex matter, and one in which some states participate much more than others. In some cases, it *can* be seen as benevolent—for example, in certain matters concerning the global environment—and in others less so—as when the governments of the highly developed countries, particularly the United States, push for worldwide market reform and privatization in developing countries.

I confine the analysis here to the economic arena, where the international role of the state has been read in rather diverse, though not necessarily mutually exclusive, ways. For instance, according to some, much of this new role of states in the global economy is dominated by the furthering of a broad neoliberal conception, to the point where it represents a constitutionalizing of this project.[42] Others emphasize that effective international participation by national governments can contribute to the strengthening of the rule of law at the global level.[43]

Yet others see the participation of the state in international systems as contributing to the loss of sovereignty. One can see this in recent debates over the World Trade Organization, fueled by concerns that it imposes restrictions on the political autonomy of the national state by

placing the principle of free trade above all other consid-
erations. For example, some fear that it will be used to
enforce the GATT trade regulations to the point of over-
turning federal, state, and local laws. This is then seen as
jeopardizing a nation's right to enact its own consumer,
labor, and environmental laws. It is worth noting here that
many in the United States who supported the GATT did not
like the role of the WTO because they did not like the idea
of binding the nation to an international dispute-resolu-
tion tribunal not fully controlled by the United States.

An important question running through these different
interpretations is whether the new transnational regimes
and institutions are creating systems that strengthen the
claims of certain actors (corporations, the large multinational legal firms) and correspondingly weaken the positions of states and smaller players. John Ruggie has
pointed out that "global markets and transnationalized
corporate structures . . . are not in the business of replac-
ing states," yet they can have the potential for producing
fundamental changes in the system of states.[44]

What matters here is that global capital has made
claims on national states, which have responded through
the production of new forms of legality. The new geography of global economic processes, the strategic territories for economic globalization, have to be defined in
terms of both the practices of corporate actors, including
the requisite infrastructure, and the work of the state in

producing or legitimating new legal regimes. Views that characterize the national state as simply losing significance fail to capture this very important fact and reduce what is happening to a function of the global-national duality: what one wins, the other loses. By contrast, I view deregulation not simply as a loss of control by the state but as a crucial mechanism for handling the juxtaposition of the interstate consensus to pursue globalization and the fact that national legal systems remain as the major, or crucial, instantiation through which guarantees of contract and property rights are enforced.

There are two distinct issues here. One is the formation of new legal regimes that negotiate between national sovereignty and the transnational practices of corporate economic actors. The second is the particular content of these new regimes, one that strengthens the advantages of certain types of economic actors and weakens those of others. Concerning governance, these two aspects translate into two different agendas. One is centered on the effort to create viable systems of coordination and order among the powerful economic actors now operating globally (to ensure, one could say, that the big boys at the top don't kill each other). International commercial arbitration and credit-rating agencies can be seen as contributing to this type of order. The second is focused less on how to create order at the top than on equity and distributive questions in the context of a globally integrated economic system with immense inequalities in the profit-making capacities of firms and the earnings capacities of households.

This second, equity-oriented agenda is further constrained by some of the order-creating governance issues arising from a global economic system increasingly dominated by finance. For now, I want to raise two larger questions of principle and politics: What actors gain legitimacy to govern the global economy and take over rules and authorities previously controlled by the national state? Do the new systems for governance that are emerging and the confinement of the role of national states in the global economy to promoting deregulation, markets, and privatization indicate a decline of international public law?[45]

I see an important parallel here. Certain components of the state's authority to protect rights are being displaced onto so-called universal human rights codes, a subject I develop in chapter 3. While the national state was and remains in many ways the guarantor of the social, political, and civil rights of a nation's people, from the 1970s on we see a significant transformation in this area. Human rights codes have become a somewhat autonomous source of authority that can delegitimize a state's particular actions if it violates such codes. Thus both the global capital market and human rights codes can extract accountability from the state, but they do so with very different agendas. Both have gained a kind of legitimacy.

It is clear that defining the nation-state and the global economy as mutually exclusive operations is, in my analysis, highly problematic. The strategic spaces where many global processes take place are often national; the mechanisms through which the new legal forms necessary for globalization are implemented are often part of state institutions; the infrastructure that makes possible the hypermobility of financial capital at the global scale is situated in various national territories. The condition of the nation-state, in my view, cannot be reduced to one of declining significance. The shrinking capacity of the state to regulate many of its industries cannot be explained simply by the fact that firms now operate in a global rather than in a national economy. The state itself has been a key agent in the implementation of global processes, and it has emerged quite altered by this participation. The form and content of participation varies between highly developed and developing countries and within each of these groupings.

Sovereignty and territory, then, remain key features of the international system. But they have been reconstituted and partly displaced onto other institutional arenas outside the state and outside the framework of nationalized territory. I argue that sovereignty has been decentered and territory partly denationalized. From a longer historical perspective, this would represent a transformation in the articulation of sovereignty and territory as they have marked the formation of the modern state and interstate system. And it would entail a need to expand the analytic terrain within which the social sciences examine some of these processes, that is to say, the explicit or implicit tendency to use the nation-state as the container of social, political, and economic processes.

The denationalization of territory occurs through both corporate practices and the as yet fragmentary ascendant new legal regime. This process does not unfold within the geographic conception of territory shared by the generals who fought the wars for nationalizing territory in earlier centuries. It is instead a denationalizing of specific institutional arenas. (Manhattan is the equivalent of a free trade zone when it comes to finance, but it is not Manhattan the geographic entity, with all its layers of activity, functions, and regulations that is a free trade zone; it is a highly specialized functional or institutional realm that has become denationalized.)

Sovereignty remains a feature of the system, but it is now located in a multiplicity of institutional arenas: the new emergent transnational private legal regimes, new supranational organizations (such as the WTO and the institutions of the European Union), and the various international human rights codes. All these institutions constrain the autonomy of national states; states operating under the rule of law are caught in a web of obligations they cannot disregard easily (though they clearly can to some extent, as is illustrated by the United States' unpaid duties to the United Nations: if this were a personal credit card debt, you or I would be in jail).

What I see is the beginning of an unbundling of sovereignty as we have known it for many centuries—but not always. Scholars examining changes in mentalities or social epistemologies have remarked that significant, epochal change frequently could not be grasped by contemporaries: the vocabularies, categories, master images available to them were unable to capture fundamental change. Suffering from the same limitations, all we see is the collapse of sovereignty as we know it. But it seems to me that rather than sovereignty eroding as a consequence of globalization and supranational organizations, it is being transformed. There is plenty of it around, but the sites for its concentration have changed over the last two decades—and economic globalization has certainly been a key factor in all this. Over the last ten or fifteen years, economic globalization has reconfigured the intersection of territoriality and sovereignty as it had been constituted over the last century, after struggles lasting many more. This reconfiguration is partial, selective, and above all strategic. Some of its repercussions for distributive justice and equity are profoundly disturbing. And even in the domain of immigration policy, where the state is still considered as absolutely sovereign, the new web of obligations and rights that states need to take into account under the rule of law in the making of policy has caused conditions to change. I discuss these issues in the following chapters.

TWO

ON ECONOMIC CITIZENSHIP

In addressing the question of how economic globalization has affected the exclusive territoriality and sovereignty that have marked the modern state, I argued that economic globalization has contributed to a denationalizing of national territory, though in a highly specialized and functional manner that befits the tenor of our era. I also argued that sovereignty, until now largely concentrated in the national state, had become somewhat decentered; there are other locations for the particular form of power and legitimacy we call sovereignty: now it is also located in supranational organizations such as the European Economic Union, the new emergent transnational legal regime, and international covenants proclaiming the universality of human rights. All of these constrain the autonomy of any state operating under the rule of law, and they do so in many distinct and divergent ways. The processes of economic globalization have played a critical role in these developments.

Now I want to address the institution of citizenship and examine the impact of a global economy on the continuity and formation of rights associated with citizenship, particularly those that grant the power to extract accountability from governments. Together with sovereignty and exclusive territoriality, citizenship marks the specificity of the modern state.

There are different views and analyses of the history of citizenship. For some (by far the majority) the origins of the institution go back to an earlier period; there were forms of citizenship in early Greece and medieval Europe, for instance. But other historians and theorists posit—quite controversially—that it is an essentially modern concept: contemporary ideas of citizenship and democracy are products of the French Revolution and its aftermath.[1] They base their analysis on the assumption that the evolution of citizenship participation is founded on a number of structural and cultural preconditions: a city culture, secularization, the decline of particularistic values, the emergence of the idea of a public realm, the erosion of particularistic commitments, and the administrative framework of the nation-state. It can also be argued that the idea of citizenship is not only modern but Western. Max Weber pointed out that it is difficult to dissociate the evolution of citizenship from the development of urban civil society; citizens were privileged members of the city-states that sprang up with the growth of European trade. But whether the concept applies in Muslim or Southeast Asian societies, for example, is a complex question.[2] In other words, having developed out of a particular conjuncture of cultural and structural conditions that may be peculiar to the West, citizenship may not be a universal concept. The universalizing of the institution, then, presupposes the possibility of mandating it from above.[3] Many non-Western nations have adopted it in their constitutions, and citizenship and civil society have become widely used in the political cultures of Asia, Africa, and Latin America.

Two logics frame my discussion here. One is that as an institution crucial to governing and accountability in national states, citizenship may also play a role in governing the global economy. It does so not simply to create order at the top but also to ensure some sort of accountability through the electoral and judicial process, this being one of the functions of citizenship in the national state. What forms this accountability might take and to what constituencies it would respond are not clear at all.

The second logic framing the analysis in this chapter is that the history of modern citizenship shows the importance of underlying conditions in shaping it.[4] Insofar as the global economy has created new conditions, it may spur another phase in the evolution of the institution of citizenship.[5]

The institution and construct of citizenship are being destabilized. First, a critical rereading of the generally accepted history of citizenship represents an alternative to the modernization assumptions underlying much analysis of citizenship, that is, the notion that as countries develop and the public sphere expands as a consequence of industrialization, modern Western-style citizenship is an inevitable outcome. Critics of this theory argue that industrialization and the rise of capitalism do not inevitably lead to the universalism and public orientation necessary for citizenship. There can be economic growth and increases in productivity, and there can be capitalism, without the particular form of modern citizenship evident especially in Europe and North America. For example, Japan and the newly industrialized countries of Asia—Singapore, Taiwan, South Korea—today still have strong family- and clan-based organizational forms in the economy. The nations of Islam had cities and a strong urban tradition, yet loyalties pushed in directions other than Western-style citizenship.

According to some, then, the constituent components of modern citizenship stand in no clear causal relation to the radically extended public sphere of industrial society. This public sphere may well be infused by such noncitizenship-like features as means-ends rational calculations of advantage, an exclusive dedication to economic activity, and the dominance of political elites.[6] (In such descriptions of the public, I recognize key aspects of the United States today.) They suggest that at least some of the scholarship on citizenship has in mind a highly specific construct that may no longer exist, given changes in contemporary conditions. The changes are such that it is questionable whether the institution, as conventionally defined, still corresponds to the earlier specification. This critique of modernization models also suggests that mandating Western-type citizenship from above will be difficult, because citizenship is at least partly culturally grounded.

This leads me to a second destabilizing force: Once we accept the cultural and historical specificity of concepts of civil society and citizenship in Western social and political theory, we need to reckon, at least theoretically, with the impact of global forces that challenge the authority of the nation-state. Thus immigrant mobility within the territory of the EC has once again brought to the fore the question of citizenship in Europe itself, the birthplace of the institution.[7] In other parts of the world, too, there are enormous problems of state membership for aboriginal communities, stateless people, and refugees. These changes have important implications for human rights in relation to citizenship.[8] As politics becomes more global, human rights will assume an expanded role in its normative regulation. What will change in that relationship?[9] Will citizenship rights be partly replaced by human rights? What institutions will enforce human rights?

The social changes in the role of the nation-state, the globalization of political issues, and the relationship between dominant and subordinate groups also have major implications for questions of membership and personal identity.[10] Is citizenship as conventionally instituted a useful concept for exploring the problems of belonging in the modern world? In a world where globalization may challenge the sovereignty of the nation-state and civil solidarity, what is the analytic terrain within which the social sciences need to examine the question of rights? Do we need to expand this terrain, to introduce new elements in the discourse?

To address these questions, I use the construct of economic citizenship to deconstruct the very notion of "citizenship," a contested construct today and, to some extent, a contested institution.[11] Economic citizenship is a strategic research site and nexus in my examination of the impact of economic globalization, a construct that destabilizes the cumulative linearity built into many histories of the institution of citizenship. Have the specific conditions brought on by economic globalization, especially in highly developed countries, contributed to yet another major transformation in the institution of citizenship? My answer is yes. But with a twist—and not a pretty one.

As mentioned, the history of citizenship shows the development of different types of citizenship rights over time. In T. H. Marshall's formulation, they are civil, political, and, most recently, social rights corresponding to the formation of the welfare state.[12] I do not want to focus on the details of this history but rather seize on its implications in order to address the question of economic globalization and its impact on the institution of citizenship today. Historicizing the institution means not stopping at the latest bundle of rights that came with the welfare state. It means recognizing the possible erosion of some of the preconditions of citizenship. Today's welfare state crises, growing unemployment, and growing earnings inequality in all the highly developed countries can certainly be read as signaling a change in the entitlements of citizens. To what extent the changes are connected to economic globalization varies from country to country and is difficult to establish with precision. But overall there is a growing consensus that the race to the bottom in the highly developed countries and the world at large is a function of global competition and that disinvestment or insufficient investment in industries that offer middle-income jobs is also partly a function of hypermobile capital in search of the most profitable short-term opportunities around the globe. Securitization and the ascendance of finance generally have further stimulated the global circulation of capital and the search for investment opportunities worldwide rather than long-term economic and social development. These investment decisions do not favor the growth of a large middle class. One of the most disturbing trends today is the vast expansion in the numbers of unemployed and never-employed people in all the highly developed countries. And masses of poor in the developing countries lack access to the means for survival. Thus, while no precise measure is available, a growing body of evidence signals that economic globalization has hit at some of the major conditions that have hitherto supported the evolution of citizenship and particularly the formation of social rights.

An emerging body of scholarship and political analysis posits that rights to economic well-being, to economic survival, should be added to the social rights that came with the welfare state.[13] Some of these studies place this claim at the heart of democratic theory, arguing that employment and economic well-being are essential conditions for democratic politics. I agree with this. But my question here does not concern the claim to economic citizenship and its legitimacy. Instead, I ask, is there currently an aggregation of economic rights that constitutes a form of economic citizenship, in that it empowers and can demand accountability from government?

My reading of the evidence is, yes, there is. But this economic citizenship does not belong to citizens. It belongs to firms and markets, particularly the global financial markets, and it is located not in individuals, not in citizens, but in global economic actors. The fact of being global gives these actors power over individual governments. This is all deeply bound up with fundamental changes brought about by economic globalization.

To examine this particular instantiation of the notion of economic citizenship I begin by outlining a set of practices, as I did in my examination of territoriality and sovereignty in the previous chapter. These are the practices firms and markets can engage in that amount to a bundle of "rights," some of them formally specified rights and others de facto permissions that flow from them. Multinationals and the global financial markets are the most powerful actors here.

The global financial markets, in particular, represent one of the most astounding aggregations of new rights and legitimacy that we have seen over the last two decades. Like the new covenants on human rights, they have taken on more of the powers historically associated with the nation-state than any other institution over the last decades. These two new contestants in the redistribution of legitimacy are enormously different from each other and have utterly different constituencies. Here I confine myself to the global financial markets; the final chapter focuses in part on human rights and the challenges posed by immigration to states under the rule of law.

The Global Capital Market

The formation of a global capital market represents a concentration of power capable of influencing national government economic policy and, by extension, other policies as well. These markets now exercise the accountability functions associated with citizenship: they can vote governments' economic policies down or in; they can force governments to take certain measures and not others. Investors vote with their feet, moving quickly in and out of countries, often with massive amounts of money. While the power of these markets is quite different from that of the political electorate, they have emerged as a sort of global, cross-border economic electorate, where the right to vote is predicated on the possibility of registering capital. Here I want to examine how they fulfill these functions and what the implications are for national economies.

The deregulation of domestic financial markets, the liberalization of international capital flows, computer networks and telecommunications have all contributed to an explosive growth in financial markets. Since 1980 the total value of financial assets has increased two and a half times faster than the aggregate GDP of all the rich industrial economies. And the volume of trading in currencies, bonds, and equities has increased about five times faster.[14] The global capital market makes it possible for money to flow anywhere regardless of national origin and boundaries, although some countries (such as Iraq) are not integrated.

The market for foreign currencies, by its very nature a cross-border market, is generally recognized to have been the first to globalize, in the mid-1970s. According to figures from the Bank for International Settlement, it is the largest financial market today and is actually global. It has gone from a daily turnover rate of about 15 billion U.S. dollars in the 1970s, to 60 billion in the early 1980s, and an estimated 1.3 trillion in 1995. In contrast, the total foreign currency reserves of the rich industrial countries amounted to only 640 billion in the early 1990s. Foreign exchange transactions were ten times larger than world trade in 1983; only ten years later, in 1992, they were sixty times larger.[15] And world trade was no slouch.

When the bond market became integrated in the 1980s, there was an explosion in cross-border bond trading. For example, total international purchases and sales of U.S. Treasury bonds—U.S. government debt—rose from 30 billion dollars in the early 1980s to 500 billion in the early 1990s. "Equity markets have been much slower to go global," a fact partly explained "by international differences in accounting practices" and restrictions on foreign holdings of equities by pension funds.[16]

Though there is no comprehensive measure of cross-border capital flows (including cross-border currency flows), the total of various separate markets approximates 75 trillion dollars. Can it grow bigger? Yes, it can. According to a 1994 study published by the McKinsey Global Institute, this is only the midpoint of a fifty-year process that will culminate in the full integration of these markets. Financial markets are expected to expand even further in relation to the size of the real economy. It is estimated that the total stock of financial assets traded in the global capital markets increased from 5 trillion dollars in 1980 to 35 trillion in 1992—twice the GDP of OECD countries, at the time the twenty-three richest industrial countries in the world. The forecast is that by the year 2000 this value will rise to 83 trillion dollars, three times the aggregate OECD's GDP.[17] Much more integration and power may lie ahead for capital markets,[18] though even now an immense amount of capital can be moved across borders at short notice.

Yet a global capital market could conceivably be nothing more than a vast pool of money for investors to play with; the power to discipline governments' economic policy making is not inherent to it. How does the massive growth of financial flows and assets and the emergence of an integrated global capital market affect states in their economic policy making? To address this question, it helps to examine how this current phase of the global capital market compares with an earlier phase, when international financial markets operated under the gold standard from the late 1800s to World War I.

In many ways the international financial market from the late 1800s to World War I was as massive as today's. This is certainly the case in terms of both its volume as a share of national economies at the time and the relative size of international flows. Capital flows dominated national economies. Monetary growth was tied to international flows of gold, leaving governments with little room for autonomy. And Keynes was railing against speculators in the financial markets just the way many of us do today. He pointed to the same type of inversion that many see happening now: that financial markets, rather than investments in production, drive economies. For Keynes, when finance dominates, "the development of the country becomes a by-product of the activities of a casino."[19]

The international capital market in that earlier period was large and dynamic, highly internationalized, and backed by a healthy dose of Pax Britannica to keep order—of a certain kind. The extent of the internationalization can be seen in the fact that in 1920, for example, Moody's rated bonds issued by about fifty governments to raise money in the U.S. capital markets. The Depression brought on a radical decline in this internationalization, and it was only very recently that Moody's once again rated the bonds of as many governments. Indeed, not until the 1980s did the international financial markets reemerge as a major factor, and as late as 1985 only fifteen foreign governments were borrowing in the U.S. capital markets.[20]

There are important differences between today's global capital market and the period of the gold standard before the First World War. The new information technologies have brought instantaneous transmission, interconnectivity, and speed to the financial markets. Gross volumes have increased enormously even when relative flows between countries are not relatively higher. The speed of transactions has brought its own consequences: trading in currencies and securities is instant, thanks to vast computer networks. And the high degree of interconnectivity in combination with instantaneous transmission signals the potential for exponential growth.

In addition, market power is now increasingly concentrated in institutions such as pension funds and insurance companies. "Institutional investors now manage almost two-fifths of U.S. households' financial assets, up from one-fifth in 1980. U.S. institutional investors' assets rose from 59 percent of GDP in 1980 to 126 percent in 1993."[21]

A third major difference is the explosion in financial innovations that have come to be referred to as "securitization." These have been enormously important in raising liquidity levels: what was thought to be nonliquid could now be traded in open markets. Though it is just beginning in most of Europe, securitization is well advanced in the United States. For instance, by 1994 the total value of derivatives—one type of innovation—sold over the counter or traded in exchanges had risen to more than 30 trillion dollars worldwide. This proliferation has furthered the linking of national markets by making it easier to exploit price differences between different financial instruments. (I should note that while currency and interest-rates derivatives did not exist until the early 1980s, derivatives on commodities—so-called futures—have been around in some version for much longer. Amsterdam's stock exchange in the seventeenth century—when it was the financial capital of the world—was based almost entirely on trading in commodity futures.)

The Global Capital Market and the State

Does the concentration of capital in unregulated markets affect national economies and government policies? Does it alter the functioning of democratic governments? Does it reshape the accountability relation between governments and their people that operates through electoral politics? Yes, it does. What are the mechanisms through which the global capital market actually exercises its disciplining function on national governments and pressures them to become accountable to the logic of these markets?

The global financial markets have affected the capacities of governments to regulate their economies. Before deregulation, governments could (to some extent) directly control the amount of bank lending through credit controls and impose ceilings on interest rates, which made monetary policy more effective than it is today. For instance, to cite a well-known case in the United States, Regulation Q imposed interest-rate ceilings and thereby protected the holdings of savings-and-loan associations by preventing their flight to higher-interest-bearing alternatives. In 1985 Regulation Q was lifted. The absence of interest-rate ceilings meant that money left the savings-and-loan associations in hordes, creating a massive slump in mortgages and housing construction.[22] When it comes to public spending, governments are increasingly subject to outside pressures.

With deregulation of interest rates in more and more highly developed countries, central banks can now only rely on changes in interest rate levels to influence the level of demand in the economy. They can no longer use interest rate ceilings. But the impact of interest rates on the economy has, in turn, been blunted by the invention and widespread use of derivatives.

Derivatives (futures, swaps, options) were invented precisely to diminish the impact of interest rate changes; they thereby reduce governments' abilities to use interest rate policy to influence the economy. Indeed, an estimated

85 percent of U.S. Fortune 500 firms "make some use of derivatives to insulate themselves from swings in interest rates and currency values,"[23] as do public-sector entities; the notorious case of Orange County in California is a prime example. Most of these derivatives are actually on interest rates, which means that as their use expands, the power of central banks to influence the economy through interest rates will decline further.[24]

The reduced sensitivity in the economy to changes in interest rates affects the impact of government borrowing on the economy. That is, before the 1980s a very high level of borrowing by the government, like that under Reagan in the 1980s, would have sent interest rates skyrocketing, making the cost of capital unbearably high and hence the level of government borrowing unacceptable to the national economy. Now this impact is diluted or much postponed. But there is no free lunch—and we are paying for it now through the reduction in the social fund.

From 1945 to 1974 total net public-sector debt as a share of GDP in the OECD economies fell steadily, down to 15 percent by 1973.[25] Since 1974 it has risen to reach 40 percent of GDP today. Under the Bretton Woods system, fixed exchange rates and restricted capital flows meant that national debt had to be financed out of official reserves. That made it impossible for governments to run big deficits (just as we couldn't before credit cards— although even with them, our free ride is shorter, and the unpleasant consequences more direct than anything the government faces). The global capital market has made it possible for governments to carry bigger debt and for some governments to do so for longer terms. This is thanks to massive innovations that transformed debt into various forms of tradable (i.e., profit-making) instruments. Any concentrated pile of money has become attractive to traders; whether it is negative (debt) or positive is now somewhat secondary. This is one of the major accomplishments of the innovations of the 1980s.

Because the financial markets have invented ways of profiting from irresponsible borrowing, they are not disciplining governments where and when it might count. But eventually, and often suddenly, markets do punish governments for excessive borrowing, forcing them to make cuts. In the meantime, they will stretch the profit-making opportunities for as long as possible, no matter what the underlying damage to the national economy might be. Investors threw money into Mexico even though its current account deficit was growing fast, reaching an enormous 8 percent of GDP in 1994. Notwithstanding recognition by critical sectors in both the United States and Mexico that the peso needed a gradual devaluation, nothing was done. But then a sudden sharp devaluation with the subsequent panicked departure of investors threw the economy into disarray. (The nationality of the investors is quite secondary, though an

IMF report says that Mexicans were the first to dump the peso.) Gradual action could probably have avoided some of the costs and reversals. Even in late 1994 many Wall Street analysts and traders were still urging investment in Mexico, and it was not till February 1995 that foreign investors began getting out in hordes. It all started with an excessive inflow and concluded with an excessive outflow.

The moral of this story is that sooner or later the price always has to be paid. In this country, many long years after the borrowing frenzy began with Reagan, the government is scrambling to find ways to pay. And Congress, following the pattern set by many other countries, has opted for disproportionate cuts in the social fund. The United States went from being the biggest creditor country in the world to being the biggest debtor. That is the long-term inheritance of the freedom to borrow in global capital markets.

The power of governments to influence interest and foreign exchange rates and fiscal policy can also be severely reduced, if not neutralized, by the foreign exchange and bond markets. For example, these markets can respond to a cut in interest rates by the U.S. government by raising the cost of loans to the government through an increased yield in long-term bonds. This has emerged as standard procedure. Then there is the famous case of George Soros and his Quantum fund, which made one billion dollars in profits on Black Wednesday in 1992 by helping to push the British pound out of the European Exchange Rate Mechanism.

There is more. Central banks have traditionally carried out their monetary policies through the banking sector. But in the United States, for instance, the weight of this sector in the economy is shrinking because of the new financial institutions and instruments developed over the last decade through deregulation. Thirty years ago banks provided three-quarters of all short- and medium-term business credit; today that proportion is down to under 50 percent. The share of commercial banks in total financial assets has dropped from more than half to just a quarter over the past seventy years.[26] The rise of electronic cash further reduces the central bankers' control over the money supply, because electronic money moves through computer networks, bypassing the information-gathering systems of central banks. Another issue is the currency markets. Governments with large debts are in fact partly in the hands of investors—whether foreign or national— who can switch their investments to other currencies. Governments and their central banks have thus been losing control over long-term interest rates, no minor matter if you consider that 60 percent or more of private-sector debt in the United States, Japan, Germany, and France is linked to them.

All of these conditions have reduced the control that central banks have over the money supply. Clearly the consequences vary in severity depending on a country's banking structure, but overall the impact of financial deregulation and innovation has been to make the effect of a change in interest rates on a national economy more uncertain and to increase the opportunities for mistakes.

There is a whole separate discussion to be had about who benefited during the period when the central banks—for example, the Federal Reserve in the United States—had greater control. But one thing is certain: even though many were excluded, the beneficiaries were from a far wider spectrum of workers, communities, and firms than they are today. Central banks and governments appear now to be increasingly concerned about pleasing the financial markets rather than setting goals for social and economic well-being; to cite just one example, after the Mexican crisis, the Argentinean and Brazilian governments promised not to devalue their currencies, no matter what the cost. In the past, inflation was a way of coping with growing debt. But today the bond markets will raise yields—and hence the cost of loans to governments— thereby sometimes terrorizing governments into keeping inflation under control. Trying to accommodate inflation-obsessed bondholders, governments impose excessive deflation on economies, at the expense of job growth.

It could be argued that there may be some positive effects as well: if a national debt becomes too large, bond-holders will demand higher yields (i.e., raise the cost of loans to governments) and lower the value of the national currency, as is clearly the case with the dollar in the United States. But this only happened after more than a decade of Reagan-Bush excessive spending on defense, and payment for the added debt has been extracted from the social fund, infrastructure, public housing construction, school buildings, parks, and so on. The dollar has plunged by 60 percent against the yen and German mark since the mid-1980s; this can be seen as a judgment on U.S. economic policies on borrowing.

Do we want the global capital market to exercise this discipline over our governments? And to do so at all costs—jobs, wages, safety, health—and without a public debate? While it is true that these markets are the result of multiple decisions by multiple investors and thus have a certain democratic aura, all the "voters" have to own capital, and small investors typically operate through institutional investors, such as pension funds, banks, and hedge funds. This leaves the vast majority of a country's citizens without any say.

The global capital market is a mechanism for pricing capital and allocating it to the most profitable opportunity. The search for the most profitable opportunities and the speedup in all transactions, including profit taking, potentially contribute to massive distortions in the flow of capital. Yes, there is a logic of sorts to the operation of markets, but it will not inevitably lead to the desirable larger social and economic investments. The issue here is not so much that global markets have emerged as a powerful mechanism through which those with capital can influence government policy; in many ways, that is an old story.[27] It is rather that the operation of these markets calls for certain types of economic policy objectives. Given the properties of the systems through which they operate—speed, simultaneity, and interconnectivity— they can produce outcomes much greater than the sum of the parts. And this weight can be brought to bear on any country integrated into the financial markets—and there are more and more of them.

A New Zone of Legitimacy?

Is the power of the global capital market a threat to democracy and to the notion that the electoral system is a way for citizens to extract accountability and ensure some control over their governments? As noted, some argue that financial markets are democratic because they reflect the opinions and decisions of millions of investors, thereby functioning as a sort of around-the-clock global opinion poll.

One scholar, Wilhelm Roepke, trying to understand the relation between international law and the international economy before World War I, under the Pax Britannica, refers to this international realm as a res publica non christiana, seeing in it a secular version of the res publica christiana of the Middle Ages. Is the transnational web of rights and protections that multinational firms and global markets enjoy today the next step in this evolution: the privatizing of an international zone that was once a res publica? Some legal scholars are positing that we are headed for a situation where international law will be predominantly international private law, that is, international economic law.[28] While in principle you and I are included under such law, in practice it largely addresses the needs and claims of firms and markets.

Although there is much to be said about this new zone of legitimacy, I want to confine myself to two observations. First, national states have participated in its formation and implementation, as I described briefly in the preceding chapter. There is a consensus among states to further the interests of economic globalization.[29] Second, the implicit ground rules of our legal system contain far more permissions than have been formalized in explicit rules of permission and prohibition.[30] This analytical elaboration can help us conceptualize the bundle of rights that has accrued to firms and markets over the last decade of economic globalization.

Do the energetic and inventive lawyers and executives who are the vanguard of this process face any hurdles in their race to economic globalization? Yes, they do.

Let me illustrate with the case of international mergers. These have been increasing rapidly over the last few years, yet the procedure remains cumbersome, a veritable obstacle course. Consider, for example, the international merger of Gillette and Wilkinson. The 1989 Gillette-Wilkinson acquisition was reviewed either formally or informally by the following agencies: the Australian Trade Practices Commission, the Brazilian Conselho Administrativo de Defesa Economica, the Canadian Bureau of Competition Policy, the European Commission, the French Conseil de la Concurrence, the German Federal Cartel Office, the Irish Fair Trade Commission, the U.S. Department of Justice, and seven other such agencies. But these obstacles are unlikely to stop the process; they are mere grist for the lawyers' mills and bills. Beyond them, however, are countervailing trends that can strengthen what is now being weakened, tools to create a different kind of governance of the global economy. They can be grouped in three broad categories.

The first category is what I think of as instruments lying on the shelf, waiting to be used. I have done research on a variety of them, even going back to some of the original formulations concerning various institutions that came out of the Bretton Woods agreements. I was after dormant potential, so to speak. The pickings were slim. But there were some.

For instance, certain features of the GATT's original document in the Bretton Woods agreement have not received sufficient, if any, attention and remain unused.[31] They happen to be about more universal issues, such as general well-being in the community of states.

There is a whole historiography to be produced here as to why certain features were left undeveloped and unactivated while others evolved into a position of ascendance. I can only focus on one particular form of this recovery here. Professor Kenneth Abbott, of Northwestern University Law School, has studied the GATT in great detail and found that most of the analyses and even debates between contrary positions have focused on what could be referred to as the "private" side of the GATT, neglecting the "public" side of the agreement.

Abbott notes that most discussions of the GATT as an institution—particularly those relating to rule making, dispute settlement, enforcement, and such—are organized around opposing conceptions. Two of these dichotomies dominate the literature, though there are variants. The most common is legalism versus pragmatism. The other dichotomy is represented by John Jackson's rule-oriented versus power-oriented procedures and diplomacy. Abbott proposes an additional dichotomy for thinking about GATT institutional issues: institutions and procedures designed to serve "private" interests and those designed to serve the "public" interest. *Public* refers here to the common interests of the nations forming the world trading community; *private* to the particular interests of the individual states, the contracting parties to the GATT. This distinction leads to intellectual connections that the GATT fraternity does not normally make; it provides perspectives on the nature of the GATT as an institution (under both its traditional arrangements and the reforms negotiated in the Uruguay Round) that differ from the traditional legalist and pragmatist positions (although they all overlap). Indeed, it reveals, according to Abbott, that both of these positions, perhaps surprisingly, operate largely on the "private" side of the dichotomy.[32]

That an important instrument such as the GATT actually contains undeveloped potential for the development of arrangements aimed at the community of states rather than simply the positions of individual states vis-à-vis each other may become an important point in my larger research project about countervailing tendencies. Can the GATT and the WTO become more "public" institutions with greater "public" functions?

The second category of countervailing force is the agencies and interests within states that go against the ascendance of the global financial markets. Yes, the international role of the state in the global economic arena has to a large extent involved furthering deregulation, strengthening markets, and pushing for privatization. But does it have to be this way? Could national states instead pursue a broader international economic agenda, one that addresses questions of equity and mechanisms for accountability among the major global economic actors?

International cooperation and multinational agreements are on the rise. The participation of national states in the global environmental arena has frequently led to the signing of multilateral agreements supporting measures to protect the environment; about a hundred major treaties and agreements have gone into effect since 1972, though not all remain in force. They may not be effective, but they do create a framework that legitimates both the international pursuit of a common good and the role of national states in that pursuit.[33] Alfred Aman notes that it is in the interest of the state to play an increasingly active role at the global level.[34] In the longer term, it is more likely that stronger legal regimes will develop globally if the global issues involved have a national regulatory counterpart. Even when such regulatory approaches use the market as a tool for compliance, they can strengthen both the rule of law (nationally and globally) and accountability. The participation of national states in new international legal regimes of this sort may contribute to the development of transnational frameworks aimed at promoting greater equity.

The third category of forces that represent countervailing power is composed of the active movements and ideologies that resist the erosion of citizenship. Most important is the universalizing of the institution. A new trend in international legal discourse conditions the international status of the state on the particular political rights central to classical liberal democracy; democratic government becomes a criterion for recognition of the state, for protection of its territorial integrity, or for its full participation in the relations among states. This is reflected in the recent U.S. and EC guidelines on the recognition of new states in Eastern Europe and the territory of the former Soviet Union. There is also a recent international legal literature that seeks to establish a basis in international law for a right to democratic governance and conditions statehood on this right.

There are two related schools of thought. One, part of an older literature that emerged with postcolonial government formation, especially in Africa, relates to a larger debate on the meaning of self-determination in postcolonial international law. It associates a state's right to self-determination with the right to representative democracy for its people. A second, newer school of thought, perhaps most prominently represented by Thomas Franck, seeks to craft a right to democratic governance from existing rights of different lineages.[35] Franck anticipates that the legitimacy of each government someday will be measured definitively by international rules and processes.

The major implications for those who are in a disadvantaged position in the current system—whether women, unemployed workers, the poor, discriminated minorities, or some other group—is that these schools of thought reject the statist model in the international system that is still prevalent today, a model that is indifferent to domestic regimes and the relationship between state and society. They reevaluate the notion that the sovereign state is the exclusive representative of its population in the international sphere and reject the notion that the state is the only actor in international law that really matters. These developments raise a question about the condition of international public law. Do the new private systems for governance and accountability and the restricted role of national states in the global economy indicate a decline of international public law? What actors gain the legitimacy for governance of the global economy and emerge as legitimate claimants to take over rules and authorities hitherto encased in the national state? As I have discussed here and in the first chapter, there is a growing role for nonstate actors, but it is going disproportionately to individuals and entities with power, whether arbitrators or global markets in finance. We need to redress that balance.

THREE

IMMIGRATION TESTS
THE NEW ORDER

Economic globalization denationalizes national economies; in contrast, immigration is renationalizing politics. There is a growing consensus in the community of states to lift border controls for the flow of capital, information, and services and, more broadly, to further globalization. But when it comes to immigrants and refugees, whether in North America, Western Europe, or Japan, the national state claims all its old splendor in asserting its sovereign right to control its borders. On this matter there is also a consensus in the community of states. One of the questions I want to examine here is the interaction between the denationalizing of key economic institutions and spaces, on the one hand, and the renationalizing of politics on the other—economic denationalizing and political renationalizing, in short. How can the state relinquish sovereignty in some realms and cling to it in others?

Beyond the facts of economic transnationalization, in dealing with immigration the state confronts the ascendant international human rights regime. Immigrants and refugees bring to the fore the tension between the protection of human rights and the protection of state sovereignty. This tension is particularly sharp in the case of undocumented immigrants, because their mere existence signifies an erosion of sovereignty. At least in part the tension originates in the state itself, in the conflict between its authority to control ingress and its obligation to protect those in its territory. Furthermore, insofar as immigrants and refugees have gained considerable rights, this can be read as a devaluation of citizenship as a condition for access to rights. Yet, as I will argue, this is a two-way process. The state has been a participant in the emergence of human rights regimes, and various components of the state have been key agents for the incorporation of human rights in domestic law, as in the United States and Germany, for instance. Thus, as I argued for the case of economic globalization, here, too, the state, especially if under the rule of law, has been transformed by its implementation of human rights regimes, both in domestic law and in international agreements. The tension between state sovereignty and international human rights should not be seen as involving an internal and an outside base: the international human rights regime operates partly inside the national state. And, as is the case with the new legal frameworks for global capital, it is this partial grounding of a transnational regime in national institutions and practices (at least in countries under the rule of law) that lends it a distinctive power and legitimacy.

In chapter 1, I posited that exclusive territoriality—a marking feature of the modern state—is being destabilized by economic globalization and that a denationalization of national territory is now in progress, though in a highly specialized institutional and functional way. In both the previous chapters, I argued that the particular combination of power and legitimacy we call sovereignty is being decentered, partly redistributed onto other entities, particularly supranational organizations, international agreements on human rights that limit state autonomy, and the emergent private international legal regime for business transactions. With all this happening, what is the basis for the usual presumption that the state has exclusive authority over the entry of non-nationals? Is the character of that exclusive authority the same as it was before the current phase of globalization and the ascendance of human rights?

Immigration is an interesting site for such a research question because, unlike electoral politics or political rhetoric, it is an arena for both deploying ideas and pursuing the day-to-day implementation and practice of policy. The idea of the nation—or, rather, the renationalizing of the nation as an idea—can be explored freely in political rhetoric, and it clearly is, more and more, all over the developed world. Such explorations can be carried pretty far as rhetoric without interfering in the day-to-day operation of government. When it comes to immigration, however, there is a daily need to process applications, accept, reject, drive to detention centers, drive from detention centers, patrol the borders, catch, fail to catch, rescue from leaking ships in the high seas and in the low seas . . . in other words, a vast, unmeasurable multiplicity of realities that unfolds on many different terrains, from borders to courthouses, from legislatures to workplaces. Unlike the idea of renationalizing the nation, immigration reality is continuously intersecting with government practices.

Unlike much of domestic politics, immigration and its associated government practices always carry the potential of becoming an item in international relations. This is reinforced in many cases by the presence of so-called ethnic lobbies, particularly in the United States but also, under different guise, in European countries and Japan. (For instance, before the current conflict in Algeria, the treatment of Algerians in France was a regular item on the agenda between France and Algeria.)

Immigration, then, has the dual property of being a central object in and a tool for the renationalizing of political discourse and being the object of government policy and practice. This can't be said about many of the ideas current in political discourse. Immigration can be seen as a strategic research site for the examination of the relation—the distance, the tension—between the idea of sovereignty as control over who enters and the constraints states encounter in making actual policy on the matter. Immigration is thus a sort of wrench one can throw into theories about sovereignty.

Let's begin with a few figures. Today there are about 120 million immigrants worldwide, an estimate that likely excludes many undocumented aliens. Only about half of these immigrants are in the rich developed countries. Similarly, of the 20 million estimated refugees, only 30 percent are in the rich developed countries; half of these are from the former Yugoslavia and live mostly in neighboring countries. Overall figures, then, are not particularly large as a share of the population of the highly developed world. I could devote a whole chapter to discussing whether open borders would markedly raise these numbers. For now, though, I will just say that large-scale international migrations are embedded in complex economic, social, and ethnic networks; highly conditioned and structured, they are by no means a free-for-all. Reality thus belies the popular dramatic images of massive invasion by the poor. Immigration is really more of a management problem than a crisis.

My analysis focuses largely on immigration in the highly developed receiving countries.[1] I use the notion of immigration policy to refer to a wide range of distinct national policies. Note, too, that it is often difficult to distinguish between immigrants and refugees, but there are separate regimes for refugees in all these countries and an international regime as well, something that can hardly be said for immigration.

The Border and the Individual as Regulatory Sites

Policies about immigration differ widely in the highly developed countries. This is perhaps most sharply captured in the criteria for naturalization. Some countries—for instance, Germany—have naturalization policies based on jus sanguinis, or descent, while others—France, for one—base theirs on jus solis, or place of birth. Some countries, among them, the United States and Sweden, facilitate citizenship acquisition; others, such as Switzerland and Japan, do not. Some, like Germany and France, have instituted explicit return migration policies, including monetary incentives, while other countries, notably the United States, hardly register the fact of return migration. Some countries—Canada and the

United States, for example—possess political cultures and identity formation processes that incorporate the fact of immigration, while in others, particularly Germany and Japan, this is not the case whatsoever.

In my reading, however, a fundamental framework roots all the immigration policies of the developed countries in a common set of conceptions about national borders and the role of the state. The purpose here is not to minimize the many differences in national policies but to underline a growing convergence in various aspects of immigration policy. The particular issues of interest are, first, this growing convergence at a time when the developed countries are finding their immigration policies increasingly ineffective, and, second, the de facto transnationalizing of immigration policy making over the last few years.

Key elements in this fundamental framework are (1) the sovereignty of the state and border control as the heart of the regulatory effort (whether on land or at airports or consulates in sending countries); and (2) an understanding of immigration as the consequence of emigrants' individual actions (the receiving country is taken as a passive agent, one not implicated in the process). Refugee policy, in contrast, recognizes additional factors as leading to outflows.[2] The framework for immigration singles out the border and the individual as the sites for regulatory enforcement.

When it comes to power over entry, the sovereignty of the state is well established by treaty law and constitutionally. The Convention of The Hague of 1930 asserted the right of the state to grant citizenship; the 1952 Convention on Refugees, which asserted that the right to leave is a universal right, remained silent on the right to entry (better silence than evident contradiction, I suppose). The status of refugees and their right not to be forcibly returned are established in international law, but there is no corresponding right of asylum; that is at the discretion of the receiving state.[3] Various human rights declarations and conventions urge states to grant asylum on humanitarian grounds, but they all recognize the absolute discretion of states. A few states—notably Germany—give those formally recognized as refugees a legal right to asylum, though these provisions are now under revision in Germany. More recently, the various agreements toward the formation of the European Union keep asserting the right of the state to control who can enter. This is quite a contrast with the assertions in the GATT, NAFTA, and the EU about the need to lift state controls over borders when it comes to the flow of capital, information, and services, as well as state controls over the domestic financial markets. While current international law imposes important limitations on the exercise of the sovereign power to control entry,[4] overall there is little disagreement as to the state's authority in this matter.[5]

On the issue of the individual as a focus for enforcement, two different operational logics are becoming evident. The one embedded in immigration policy, particularly in developed countries, places exclusive responsibility for the immigration process on the individual and hence makes the individual the site for the exercise of the state's authority. Yet it is now increasingly recognized that international migrations are a function of larger geopolitical and transnational economic dynamics. The worldwide evidence reveals that there is a pattern in the geography of migrations and shows that the major receiving countries tend to get immigrants from their zones of influence (this holds for countries as diverse as the United States, France, and Japan). This suggests that, because of economic internationalization and the geopolitics resulting from older colonial patterns, the responsibility for immigration may not be exclusively the immigrant's. Analytically, these conditions can enter into theorizations about the state and immigration only when we suspend the proposition implicit in much immigration analysis that immigration is the result of individual action.

The other operational logic is centered on the international human rights regime, where the individual is not the site for punishment but for legitimate rights. I return to this subject in a later section.

Beyond Sovereignty: Constraints on States' Policy Making

But how much control does the state have over immigration? An emerging de facto regime, centered in international agreements and conventions as well as in various rights gained by immigrants, limits the state's role in controlling immigration. An example of such an agreement is the International Convention adopted by the General Assembly of the UN on December 18, 1990, on the protection of the rights of all migrant workers and members of their families [Resolution 45/158].[6] Legal authorities now widely uphold a set of rights for resident immigrants. For instance, administrative and constitutional courts blocked attempts by the French and German legislatures to limit family reunification, on the grounds that such restrictions would violate international agreements. The courts have also regularly supported a combination of rights that have the effect of limiting governments' power over resident immigrants. Similarly, they have limited the ability of governments to restrict or stop asylum seekers from entering the country.[7] Over the last three decades civil and social rights have gradually expanded to include marginal populations, whether women, ethnic minorities, or immigrants and refugees.

Lobbying by interest groups has become a key ingredient in immigration policy making in the United States. The 1986 Immigration Reform and Control Act (IRCA) represents a balancing of interests that ended up limiting the effectiveness of the law. Interest groups influenced the drafting of the law and its subsequent implementation. Some INS regulations were liberalized—for example, those regarding legalization conditions—as a consequence of court action by interest groups.

Another form of this confinement of state action is illustrated by the impact of the 1975 Helsinki Accords requiring that barriers to the free movement of people and ideas be lowered. The United States had to soften regulations that were seen as violating the accords. Thus the Foreign Relations Authorization Act, passed in 1977, required the secretary of state to recommend that aliens excluded for political reasons be admitted unless this was determined to be contrary to U.S. security interests. The Moynihan-Frank Amendment of 1987 prohibited the exclusion or deportation of aliens because of political beliefs and actions that, if engaged in by a U.S. citizen, would be protected by the Constitution. Yet another example is the 1980 Refugee Act, which was predicated on the UN protocol on refugees and greatly opened the country to refugee claims.

The numbers and kinds of political actors involved in immigration policy debates and policy making in Western Europe, North America, and Japan are also far greater than they were two decades ago: the European Union; anti-immigrant parties; vast networks of organizations in both Europe and North America that often represent immigrants—or claim to do so—and fight for immigrant rights; immigrant associations and immigrant politicians, mostly in the second generation; and, especially in the United States, so-called ethnic lobbies.[8] The policy process for immigration was probably never confined to a narrow governmental arena of ministerial and administrative interaction, but today more than two decades of public opinion and public political debate have become part of the arena wherein immigration policy is shaped.[9] Whole parties position themselves politically in terms of their stand on immigration, especially in some of the European countries.

The overall effect of these developments is to constrain the sovereignty of the state and to undermine old notions about immigration control. This is particularly evident in the European Union,[10] where the single-market program has raised various issues associated with the free circulation of people as an essential element in creating a frontier-free community and the attendant problems for national immigration laws regarding non-EC nationals in EC member states. Though lacking the legal competence to deal with many of these issues, EC institutions had to begin to address them. Gradually, they became more deeply involved with visa policy, family reunification, and migration policy. Governments first resisted EC involvement in these once exclusively national domains. But now, notwithstanding many public pronouncements to the contrary, both legal and practical issues have made such involvement acceptable and inevitable, especially in the aftermath of the collapse of the socialist bloc and the rapid increase in refugees. Though very slowly, the general direction has been toward a closer union of member states' immigration policies.

In the United States, the combination of forces at the governmental level is quite different yet has similar general implications about the state's constraints in immigration policy making. When the Department of Labor (DOL) was created in 1914, it assumed responsibility for immigration policy. In June 1933 President Roosevelt combined those functions into the Immigration and Naturalization Service within DOL. The advent of World War II brought a shift in the administrative responsibility for immigration policy: in 1940 Roosevelt recommended it be transferred to the Department of Justice, because of the supposed political threat represented by immigrants from enemy countries. This was meant to last only for the duration of war. But in the late 1940s and 1950s there was great concern over how immigration policy could be used to advance foreign policy objectives. The INS was never returned to the DOL. This meant that in Congress immigration wound up in committees traditionally reserved for lawyers, such as the Senate and House Judiciary Committees. It has been said that this is why immigration law is so complicated (and, I would add, so centered on the legalities of entry and so unconcerned with broader issues).

Today jurisdiction over immigration matters in the U.S. Congress continues to lie with the Judiciary Committee, not with the Foreign Affairs Committee, as might have been the case. Congressional intent is often at odds with the foreign affairs priorities of the executive; there is a policy-making tug of war.[11] Because immigration policy in the United States is largely debated and shaped by Congress, it is subject to a vast multiplicity of local interests, notably ethnic lobbies—and we all know how sensitive congressmen and women are to the demographics of their districts. This has made the process very public, quite different from other processes of policy making.[12]

That immigration in the United States has historically been the preserve of the federal government, particularly Congress, assumes new meaning in today's context of radical devolution: the return of powers to the states.[13] Conflict has emerged between several state governments and the federal government over the particular issue of federal mandates concerning immigrants—such as access to public health care and schools—without mandatory federal funding. States with disproportionate shares of immigrants are asserting that they are disproportionately burdened by the putative costs of immigration—although the latest study by the Washington-based

Urban Institute found that immigrants contribute 30 billion U.S. dollars more in taxes than they take in services. (I should note, however, that in the United States the costs of immigration are an area of great debate and wide-ranging estimates.) At the heart of this conflict is the fact that the federal government sets policy but does not assume responsibility, financial or otherwise, for the implementation of many key aspects of immigration policy. The conflict is illustrated by the notorious case of the state of California and its 377-million-dollar lawsuit against the federal government.

The question raised by these developments is not so much about how effective a state's control is over its borders—we know it is never absolute. Rather, it concerns the substantive nature of state control over immigration given international human rights agreements, the extension of various social and political rights to resident immigrants over the last twenty years, and the multiplication of political actors involved with the immigration question. There is, first, the matter of the unintended consequences of policies, whether immigration policies as such or other policies that have immigration impacts. For instance, the 1965 U.S. Immigration Act had consequences not intended or foreseen by its framers; there was a generalized expectation it would bring in more of the nationalities already present in the country—that is, Europeans—given its emphasis on family reunion.[14] (It did not.) Other kinds of unintended migrations are those related to the internationalization of production.[15] And although immigration policy has rarely been an explicit, formal component of the foreign policy apparatus in the United States, foreign and military aid have rarely deterred emigration. On the contrary. Refugee flows from Indochina are an obvious example, but consider, too, the case of El Salvador in the 1980s: billions of dollars poured in, and hundreds of thousands of Salvadorans poured out as U.S. aid raised the effectiveness of El Salvador's military control and aggression against its own people.[16] Or take the Philippines, a country that received massive aid and has had high emigration. In both cases, the foreign aid was dictated by security issues. U.S. economic and political interventions also played a role in the Dominican emigration in the 1960s and in the emigration from India and Pakistan. (I have long argued that policymakers should attach migration impact statements to various policies having to do with overseas activities, from foreign direct investment to military aid.)

Domestic U.S. policies that have impact overseas have also contributed to promote emigration to the United States. A good example is the notorious sugar price support provision of the early 1980s: Taxpayers paid 3 billion dollars annually to support the price of sugar for U.S. producers. This kept Caribbean Basin countries out of the competition and resulted in a loss of 400,000 jobs there from 1982 to 1988 (the Dominican Republic alone lost three-quarters of its sugar export quota in less than a decade). Predictably, the 1980s was also an era of large increases in immigration to the United States from that region.

A second condition illuminating the issue of the substantive nature of state control over immigration involves a zero-sum argument: if a government closes one kind of entry category, recent history shows that numbers will increase in another. A variant on this dynamic is that if a government has, for instance, a very liberal policy on asylum, public opinion may turn against all asylum seekers and close up the country totally; this in turn is likely to promote an increase in irregular entries. It is becoming increasingly evident that unilateral policy in major immigration countries is problematic. Germany is a dramatic example: that country began to receive massive numbers of entrants as the other European states gradually tightened their policies while its asylum policy remained very liberal. And the EC today stresses the importance to the EU as a whole of the Mediterranean countries—Italy, Spain, and Portugal—maintaining control over their borders to exclude non-EC entrants.

All these constraints on the state's capacity to control immigration should not be seen as a control crisis. In fact, it seems to me that the fears of such a crisis common in many highly developed countries today are in some ways unwarranted, even though states have less control than they would like. A look at the characteristics of immigrations over time and across the world reveals that flows are highly patterned, contingent on other dynamics that contain equilibrating mechanisms; that they tend to have fixed durations (many immigrations lasted for fifty years and then came to an end); that there is more return migration than is generally recognized (for example, Soviet engineers and intellectuals going back to Moscow from Israel; Mexicans returning home after becoming legal U.S. residents through the IRCA amnesty program because they could now move freely between the two countries). Examination of earlier historical periods when there were no controls also shows that most people then did not leave poorer areas to go to richer ones, even though there were plenty of such opportunities in Europe within reasonable travel distances.[17]

Yet another set of conditions, mentioned earlier, reduces the autonomy of the state in controlling immigration: Large-scale international migrations are highly conditioned and structured, embedded in complex economic, social, and ethnic networks. States may insist on treating immigration as the aggregate outcome of individual actions, but they cannot escape the consequences of those larger dynamics. A national state may have the power to write the text of an immigration policy, but it is likely to be dealing with complex, transnational processes that it can only partly address or regulate through immigration policy as conventionally understood.

Beyond the Individual:
Economic Internationalization and Geopolitical Links

Each country is unique, and each migration is produced by specific conditions of time and place. But to theorize about the impact of economic internationalization we must step back from these particulars to examine more general tendencies in economic dominance and the formation of transnational spaces for economic activity. The goal is to grasp the impact of the internationalization of economies on, first, the mechanisms connecting emigration and immigration countries and, second, the organization of labor markets in both types of countries.

These two in turn have an impact on the formation and direction of migration flows. They produce conditions under which poverty, unemployment, or lack of opportunities for advancement can become activated as migration push factors. For example, the development of commercial agriculture and export-oriented standardized manufacturing have dislocated traditional economies and eliminated small producers. They also contribute to the conditions under which immigrants can enter the labor markets of receiving countries. For example, increased competitive pressures from the internationalization of production cause businesses to favor low-wage workers at the expense of unions, in order to remain competitive with cheap third-world imports.

The mechanisms binding immigration countries to emigration countries can assume many forms. But two appear to be dominant. One is past colonial and current neo- or quasi-colonial bonds, which can generate the types of military actions the United States has taken in El Salvador or the Philippines. The other mechanism is the economic links brought about by internationalization, ranging from the off-shoring of production, to the implantation of export-oriented agriculture by means of foreign investment, to the power of multinationals in the consumer markets of sending countries.

A third type of link, characterized by greater specificity and a variety of mechanisms, is the organized recruitment of workers, either directly by a government (within the framework of government-supported employer initiatives) or through kinship and family networks. Ethnic links established between communities of origin and destination, typically by transnational households or broader kinship structures, are crucial after a flow has begun, and ensure its persistence. These recruitment and ethnic links tend to operate within the broader transnational spaces created by neocolonial processes and/or economic internationalization.

It is a little-known fact that, during the 1800s as well as today, some form of organized recruitment by employers or governments often stimulated immigrant flows. But eventually most migration flows become independent of organized recruitment. Although organized recruitment, and with it the constitution of certain countries as labor-exporting, is radically different from the migrations engendered by former colonial bonds, similarities also exist.

The mass migrations of the 1800s formed part of a trans-atlantic economic system binding several nations by economic transactions and wars. These mass migrations were highly important to U.S. development. Massive flows of capital, goods, workers, and specific structures produced the American economic system. Earlier movements of labor across the Atlantic had largely been forced, notably through slavery, and mostly from colonized African and Asian territories. Similarly, the migrations to England of the 1950s originated in what had been British territories. Finally, the migrations into Western Europe of the 1960s and 1970s were initiated by recruitment (in a context of European regional dominance) in the Mediterranean and some Eastern European countries. Few if any passive bystanders can be found among countries receiving large influxes of laborers.

The renewal of mass immigration into the United States in the 1960s, after a hiatus of five decades, occurred during a period of expanded U.S. economic and military activity in Asia and the Caribbean Basin. The United

States is at the heart of an international system of investment and production that connects these various regions.
In the 1960s and 1970s it played a crucial role in the development of a world economic system. The U.S. passed leg-
islation aimed at opening its own and other countries'
economies to the flow of capital, goods, services, and
information. This central military, political, and economic role contributed, I argue, both to the creation of
conditions that mobilized people into migrations, whether
local or international, and to the formation of links with
the United States that subsequently served as often unintended bridges for international migration. Measures
commonly thought to deter emigration—foreign investment and the promotion of export-oriented growth in
developing countries—seem to have had the opposite
effect. Among the leading suppliers of immigrants to the
United States in the 1970s and 1980s were several newly
industrialized countries of South and Southeast Asia
whose high growth rates are generally recognized to
be a result initially of foreign investment in export manufacturing.

That migrations are patterned is further reflected in figures on the U.S. share of global immigration. Though
inadequate, the evidence compiled by the *United Nations
Demographic Yearbook* and *World Population Prospects*
shows that in the mid-1980s the United States received
about 19 percent of global emigration. This figure is

derived from data on permanent settlement, which excludes illegal immigration and unofficial refugee flows between countries, a growing category. A breakdown by region and country of origin shows a distinct pattern. The United States received 27 percent of total Asian emigration but 81.5 percent of all Korean emigration and nearly 100 percent of emigration from the Philippines. It received 70 percent of Caribbean emigration but almost 100 percent of emigration from the Dominican Republic and Jamaica and 62 percent from Haiti. And it received 19.5 percent of all emigration from Central America but 52 percent of emigration from El Salvador, the country in the region with the greatest U.S. involvement.

One could generalize from these tendencies that immigration flows take place within specific systems. The economic ties outlined here represent one possibility. In other cases, the system within which immigration takes place is political or ethnic. One could ask, for example, if systemic links underlie the current Central European migrations to Germany and Austria. Rather than the push factors of poverty and unemployment and the general failure of socialism, other links may operate as bridges. This seems likely given that both Berlin and Vienna before World War II received large migrations from a vast eastern region. Thus migration systems were produced and reproduced. In addition, the aggressive campaign during the cold war to depict the West as a place where economic well-being is the norm and well-paying jobs are easy to get must also have induced people to migrate westward. A more accurate portrayal of conditions in the West might have deterred migrants who were not determined to come at any cost. These historical and current conditions define the systems within which post-1990 eastern migration to Germany and Austria is taking place.

The claim that there is a geopolitics of migration is supported by some of the immigration patterns in Europe. Sixty percent of foreign residents in the United Kingdom are from Asian or African countries that were former dominions or colonies; European immigrants are relatively few, and almost three-quarters of them come from Ireland, another former colony. Almost no immigrants come from Turkey or Yugoslavia, which provide the largest share to Germany. Almost all immigrants to Europe from the Indian subcontinent and from the English Caribbean live in the United Kingdom.

In the ten years following World War II, a vast majority of so-called immigrants to West Germany were the eight million displaced ethnic Germans who resettled there. Another three million came from the GDR before the Berlin Wall was erected in 1961. Almost all ethnic Germans went to Germany, and those who did not went overseas. But 86 percent of Greek immigrants in Europe, almost 80 percent of Turkish immigrants, and 76 percent of Yugoslavs, also reside in Germany.

Almost all Algerians in Europe reside in France, as do 86 percent of Tunisians and 61 percent of Moroccans. Almost all immigrants in Europe from overseas territories still under French control—such as the French Antilles, Tahiti, and French Guiana—live in France. But so do 84 percent of Portuguese and Spaniards who dwell in Europe outside their countries of origin. France has a long history—going back to the 1800s—of recruiting and receiving migrant workers for its vineyards from these countries.

The Netherlands and Belgium both hosted significant numbers of immigrants from their former colonial empires. They also received foreign workers from what had emerged as labor-exporting countries such as Italy, Morocco, and Turkey. Similarly, workers immigrate to Switzerland from traditional labor-exporting countries: Italy, Spain, Portugal, Yugoslavia, and Turkey. All three countries originally recruited these workers, until eventually a somewhat autonomous set of flows was in place. Sweden receives 93 percent of Finnish immigrants and is expanding its recruitment area to include workers from the traditional labor-exporting countries on the Mediterranean.

As a labor migration flow ages, its destinations tend to become more diverse. A limited autonomy from older colonial and neocolonial bonds develops. Immigrants from Italy and Spain are now distributed among several countries. One-third of Italian immigrants in Europe reside in Germany, 27 percent in France, 24 percent in Switzerland, and 15 percent in Belgium. That destinations continue to be limited, however, signals the presence of migration systems rather than mere individual choices. More recent labor migrations still show very high levels of geographic concentration. Turks make up the largest single immigrant group in any of Europe's labor-receiving countries today, with 1.5 million in Germany.

It seems that once an area becomes a significant exporter of labor it does not easily catch up in development with labor-importing areas precisely because the latter have high, or relatively high, growth. Advantage appears to accumulate. History suggests that labor-sending areas cannot attain or are structurally unable to participate in such advantage because the spatial pattern of growth is uneven. Although generalizations are dangerous, it is clear that Italy and Ireland, which now receive immigrants, have for two centuries been labor exporters and that this has not been a macroeconomic advantage, even though individuals and localities may have benefited.

The case of Japan is interesting here. It reveals the intersection of economic internationalization and the beginning of immigration in a country with a radically different history, culture, and, to a lesser extent, economic organization from those of other advanced economies.[18]

One evident difference is Japan's lack of an immigration history. However, Japan now has a growing unauthorized immigrant workforce filling low-wage, unskilled jobs that Japanese youth reject. Processes long since established in the United States and Western Europe are becoming apparent there.

Why is this happening now rather than during the 1950s and 1960s, the period of rapid economic growth when Japan experienced sharp labor shortages? Japan is a major presence in a regional Asian economic system where it is the leading investor, foreign-aid donor, and exporter of consumer goods (including cultural products). And while Japan is not as open to foreign firms as the United States is, such businesses are increasingly common.

Is the new immigration to Japan related to these processes of internationalization? I have argued before that this trend is part of the globalization of Japan's economy.[19] It is easy to recognize in the case of high-level foreign manpower in Tokyo's financial industry. It is less clearly manifested in the new, mostly unauthorized immigration of manual workers, who are employed in construction, manufacturing, and low-wage service jobs. There, internationalization is the context in which bridges are built to the homelands of potential emigrants and contributes to making the Japanese economy more porous, particularly in Tokyo, Yokohama, and Osaka, where most immigrant workers, including the undocumented, are concentrated.

Discussions of immigration policy customarily treat the flow of labor as the result of individual actions, particularly the individual's decision to migrate in search of better opportunities. Such a view puts all the responsibility for immigration on immigrants. Commentators who speak of an immigrant "influx" or "invasion" treat the receiving country as passive: immigration is unconnected to the past or current actions of receiving countries, and immigration policy is portrayed as more or less benevolent toward immigrants. Absent is any awareness that the international activities of the governments or firms of countries receiving immigrants may have contributed to the formation of economic links with emigration countries, links that may invite the movement of people as well as capital.

Similar migration processes are now forming in all major advanced economies at the intersection of economic internationalization with labor markets. Locating the origin of immigration flows and their continuation here points up important parallels in advanced economies whose history and culture differ significantly. The parallels result from their transnational economic influence and from the economic restructuring evident in all advanced economies in the 1980s. The differences stem from the specifics of each country's culture and history.

Implications for Immigration Policy

In all the highly developed countries (and in many of the developing countries), the state has participated in constructing a global economic system and furthering a consensus to pursue this objective. This participation has affected the power of different agencies within the state and advanced the internationalization of the interstate system. Thus, although the state continues to play the most important role in immigration policy making and implementing, it is no longer sufficient simply to examine its formal role in this arena; it is also necessary to examine the transformations of both the state itself and the interstate system and what these changes can entail for migration policy and the regulation of migration flows and settlement.

There is some consensus among policymakers and scholars that a growing gap exists between immigration policy intent and immigration reality in the major developed receiving countries.[20] One possible explanation for this gap is that the limited effectiveness of immigration policy today is partly due to its neglect of these transformations in the larger context of international migration and the institutional apparatus for its regulation. Immigration policy continues to be characterized by its formal isolation from other major processes, as if it were possible to handle migration as a bounded, closed event. States' internationally recognized powers to police their frontiers and to control admission to and exclusion from their territories do not necessarily guarantee state insularity.[21]

Current immigration policy in the highly developed countries is increasingly at odds with other major policy frameworks in the international system. There is a combination of drives to create border-free economic spaces yet intensify border control to keep immigrants and refugees out. The juxtaposition between these two dynamics provides one of the principal contexts in which today's efforts to stop immigration assume their significance. There are, in effect, two major epistemic communities: one dealing with the flow of capital and information; the other with immigration. Both are international, and both enjoy widespread consensus in the community of states.

The coexistence of such different regimes for capital and for immigrants has not been seen as an issue in the United States. For this reason, the case of the EU is of more interest here: it represents an advanced stage of formalization, and European states are discovering the difficulties if not impossibility of maintaining two such diverse regimes. The European Community and the national governments of the member states struggled to handle the juxtaposition of the divergent regimes for immigration flows, on the one hand, and all other types of flows, on the other. The discussion, design, and implementation of policy aimed at forming a European

Union make it evident that immigration policy has to accommodate the facts of rapid economic internationalization. The other major regional systems in the world are far from facing this contradiction in designing their formal policy frameworks, and they may never do so, yet even they must reconcile the conflicting requirements of border-free economies and border controls to keep immigrants out. NAFTA is one such instance, as are, in a more diffuse way, various other initiatives for greater economic integration in the Western Hemisphere. There are also the regional systems constituted partly as zones of influence of major economic or geopolitical powers, such as the long-term dominance of the United States over the Caribbean Basin. The quasi-transnational economic integration characterizing such systems produces its own contradictions between drives for border-free economic spaces and border control to keep immigrants and refugees out.

There are strategic sites where it becomes clear that the existence of two very different regimes for the circulation of capital and the circulation of immigrants poses problems that cannot be solved through the old rules of the game, where the facts of transnationalization weigh in on the state's decisions regarding immigration. One example relates to the need to create special systems to govern the circulation of service workers within both the GATT and NAFTA as part of the further internationalization of trade and investment in services. Much of what we call international trade and investment in services actually involves specialized service workers; they embody the service and need to cross borders to deliver it. Hence provisions must be made for their international circulation. These labor circulation systems have been uncoupled from any notion of migration, even though they involve a version of temporary labor migration, and they are in good part under the oversight of entities that are quite autonomous from the government. Another instance can be seen in Japan's new immigration law, passed in 1990 (actually an amendment on an earlier law on the entry and exit of aliens), which opened the country to several categories of highly specialized professionals with Western backgrounds (e.g., experts in international finance, Western-style accounting, Western medicine, etc.) and made the entry of what is referred to as "simple labor" illegal.[22] In other words, the law permits the importation of the commodity "Western human capital" but closes the borders to traditional immigrants.

Human Rights and State Sovereignty

Against this web of obligations and in view of the multiplying actors involved in the immigration debate and policy world, one development emerges as singularly important for understanding the impact of immigration on questions of sovereignty and territoriality. This is the emergent international human rights regime. Human rights are not dependent on nationality, unlike political, social, and civil rights, which are predicated on the distinction between national and alien. Human rights override such distinctions and hence can be seen as potentially contesting state sovereignty and devaluing citizenship.

International human rights, while partly rooted in the founding documents of certain nation-states, are today a force that can undermine the exclusive authority of the state over its nationals and thereby contribute to transforming the interstate system and international legal order. Membership in territorially exclusive nation-states ceases to be the only ground for the realization of rights. All residents, whether citizens or not, can claim their human rights.[23] Human rights begin to impinge on the principle of nation-based citizenship and the boundaries of the nation. How does immigration fit into this, particularly undocumented immigration, which carries with it a de facto erosion of the state's sovereign power to control ingress? This is a complex question that I can only begin to address here. First, let me examine some of the instruments available and the actual possibilities for individuals and nonstate actors to use these instruments.

The concept of inalienable rights of the individual as a universal principle was already present in the French and American revolutions. Central to its interpretation was the notion that such rights could be safeguarded and realized only within the context of a nation-state. References to inalienable cross-national rights in the founding documents of nation-states were highly abstract. Already in the early twentieth century, several legal instruments promoted human rights and made the individual an object of international law. But elaboration and formalization of these rights did not occur until after World War II. The covenants and conventions that guarantee human rights today are derived from the Universal Declaration of Human Rights adopted by the UN in 1948. The formulation of human rights is partly drawn from the Declaration of Independence, the U.S. Constitution, and the Declaration of the Rights of Man and Citizen.[24]

To what extent can individuals and nonstate groups make claims on the state, particularly in the United States and Western Europe, where the human rights regime is most developed? The Universal Declaration of Human Rights is not an international treaty and thus is not legally binding. But because it is so often cited many consider it to have the status of customary international law, an international and general practice that is accepted and observed as law. The International Covenant on Civil and Political Rights and the International Covenant on Economic, Social, and Cultural Rights legislated much of what the Universal Declaration called for. Ratification procedures started in 1966, but it was ten years before thirty-five states ratified the covenants, the number required to make them legally binding. In 1976 a Protocol to the Covenant on Civil and Political Rights was opened for ratification; it enables private parties to file complaints to the UN Human Rights committee if a state that has ratified the protocol has violated its dictates. Other UN human rights treaties include the Convention on the Prevention and Punishment of Genocide (1948), the International Convention on the Elimination of All Forms of Racial Discrimination (1965), and the Convention on the Political Rights of Women (1981). These instruments are only binding on states that have ratified them, although some instruments have taken on the character of international customary law and are binding on all states.

There are also regional conventions. The European Convention on Human Rights, adopted in 1950, was established by the member states of the Council of Europe to fulfill the goals of the Universal Declaration. The inter-American system for the protection of human rights, the Inter-American Commission on Human Rights, is grounded on two distinct legal documents: the Charter of the Organization of American States and the American Convention on Human Rights, which were both adopted in 1969 and entered into force in 1978. The human rights regime of the OAS was markedly strengthened in a 1967 protocol that came into force in 1970.

In the earlier postwar phase of the elaboration of human rights instruments, the state was still the object and subject of international law. It was up to a state to lodge complaints about human rights violations to the UN or pertinent regional organs. In many ways these instruments lacked weight and influence. By the 1970s a marked transformation became evident. More instruments were available, and they started to be used more frequently; human rights activists also mention the strong support of high-ranking politicians, such as presidents Carter (United States), Arias (Costa Rica), and Alfonsin (Argentina), as well as the growing integration of communications media across the globe, which facilitates instantaneous reporting of violations. Increasingly, individuals and nonstate actors petitioned governments on the basis of international human rights codes or regional instruments, and these instruments became partly independent of the states themselves even though they were grounded in interstate agreements. This growing authority of human rights law is particularly evident in Europe. It was not until the 1980s that such law began to exert significant influence in the United States, where it still does not carry the weight it has in Europe.

The European Convention on Human Rights has taken on considerable importance. As with other human rights instruments, it bestows rights on "persons" rather than citizens, and declares that the enjoyment of rights and freedoms it contains do not depend on, among other criteria, national origin. However, the convention does not prohibit distinctions between nationals or citizens and aliens. Provisions in the convention and in the Court of Human Rights rules authorize individuals and nonstate actors to petition. Such cases increased rapidly in the 1970s and 1980s.[25] Several states have incorporated many of the convention's provisions into their domestic law, among them, Germany, Netherlands, France, Spain, Switzerland, and Turkey. In these cases, decisions by the court have a direct effect on domestic judiciaries, which emerge as key organs for the implementation of human rights provisions. This pattern has grown markedly since the early 1980s with the growth of court case law.

In the United States, this process has been much slower and less marked. This is partly due to U.S. definitions of nationhood, which have led courts in some cases to address the matter of undocumented immigrants within U.S. constitutionalism, notably the idea of inalienable and natural rights of people and persons, without territorial confines. The emphasis on persons permits interpretations about undocumented immigrants that would not be possible if the emphasis were on citizens. It was not until the mid-1970s and early 1980s that domestic courts began to consider human rights codes as normative instruments in their own right. The rapid growth of undocumented immigration and the sense that the state was incapable of controlling the flow and regulating the various categories of immigrants was a factor leading courts to consider the international human rights regime: it allows courts to rule on basic protections of individuals not formally covered in the national territory and legal system, notably undocumented aliens and unauthorized refugees.[26]

Several court cases show how undocumented immigration creates legal voids that are increasingly filled by invoking human rights covenants.[27] In many of these cases, individual or nonstate actors bring claims based on the notion of international human rights codes as expanding international law. The state, in this case the judiciary, "mediates between these agents and the international legal order."[28] Courts have emerged as central institutions for a whole series of changes.[29]

Perhaps one of the most important documents seeking to protect the rights of migrants is the 1990 International Convention on the Protection of the Rights of All Migrant Workers and Members of Their Families adopted by the General Assembly of the UN in 1990.[30] It took a decade to elaborate and approve this convention. It also contains a broad range of explicit human rights protections for undocumented migrants and members of their families to an extent not seen before in other instruments, with the exception of an International Labor Organization convention that guaranteed equality of treatment for undocumented workers in various employment-related matters; this agreement, however, covered only past employment.[31]

Immigration, Human Rights, and State Sovereignty

The growing accountability of the state to international human rights codes and institutions, together with the fact that individuals and nonstate actors can make claims on states based on those codes, signals a development that goes beyond the expansion of human rights within the framework of nation-states. It contributes to a redefinition of the bases of the legitimacy of states under the rule of law and the notion of nationality.

From an exclusive emphasis on the sovereignty of the people and right to self-determination, a shift to rights of individuals regardless of nationality has occurred. Human rights codes can thus erode the legitimacy of the state if states fail to respect such human rights. It is no longer just a question of self-determination but of respect for international human rights codes. The extent to which the organizations and instruments that privilege these individual rights are likely to be implemented is uncertain. One interpretation views these developments as indicating that international law today makes the individual and nonstate groups subsidiary to the laws between states.

In accumulating social, civic, and even some political rights in countries of residence, immigrants have diluted the meaning of citizenship and the specialness of the claims citizens can make on the state. When it comes to social services (education, health insurance, welfare, unemployment benefits) citizenship status is of minor importance in the United States and Western Europe. What matters is residence and legal alien status. Most of these countries will pay retirement benefits even if recipients no longer reside there. Some countries—for instance, Sweden and the Netherlands—have also granted local voting rights. EU immigrants have the right to vote in European parliamentary elections, but non-EU immigrants do not. Aliens are guaranteed full civil rights either constitutionally or by statute. Given the little difference between the claims that citizens and immigrants can make, immigrants have little incentive to seek naturalization.

Even unauthorized immigrants can make some of these claims. Peter Schuck has noted that new social contracts between undocumented aliens and society-at-large are being negotiated in the United States every day, contracts that cannot be nullified through claims concerning nationality and sovereignty. Courts have had to accept the existence of undocumented aliens and to extend to these aliens some form of legal recognition and guarantees of basic rights. Various decisions have conferred important benefits of citizenship upon undocumented aliens. This clearly undermines older notions of sovereignty. At the same time, California's Proposition 187 signals the possibility of reversals in this arena. Although Proposition 187 will be challenged in the courts, its success at the polls signals the political/legal potential for anti-immigrant sentiment.

For scholars who see in the new international human rights regime a major political development,[32] the erosion in the distinction between citizen and alien also devalues the institution of citizenship.[33] This devaluing may well contribute in turn to the burgeoning importance of international human rights codes. The growing ability of NGOs and individuals to make claims on the basis of international human rights instruments has implications beyond the boundaries of individual states. It affects the configuration of the international order.

The concept of nationality is being partly displaced from a principle that reinforces state sovereignty and self-determination (through the state's right/power to define its nationals) to a concept emphasizing that the state is accountable to all its residents on the basis of international human rights law. The individual emerges as the object of international law and institutions. International law still protects sovereignty and has in the state its main object, but the state is no longer the only subject of international law. In addition to all its other functions, it becomes an institutional apparatus of a transnational order based on human rights. In this process, the relationships among nongovernment entities, the state, and international institutions is reconfigured. Individuals and NGOs can make claims on the state—the one where they reside or another—and they participate in the debates and actions concerning the international legal order. That the state's jurisdictional and judicial role and its relation to the individual and nonstate actors are, in some regards, becoming organized by the international human rights legal order is clearly not an irreversible trend, as current events in the former Yugoslavia indicate, but this change does create new conditions that any international legal order must accommodate. Even strong nationalist or ethnic resistance must confront the undeniable existence of the international human rights regime.

These and other developments point to an institutional re-shuffling of some of the components of sovereign power over entry and can be seen as an extension of the general processes whereby state sovereignty is being partly decentered onto non- or quasi-governmental entities for the governance of the global economy and international political order. Put simply, these developments reduce the autonomy of the state in immigration policy making and multiply the sectors within the state that are addressing immigration policy, thereby multiplying the opportunities for conflicts within the state. Immigration policy is now shaped by forces ranging from economic globalization to international agreements on human rights, and it is made and implemented within settings ranging from national and local legislatures and judiciaries to supranational organizations.

Policy making regarding international issues has always engaged different parts of the government. Each state is constituted through multiple agencies and social forces. Indeed, it could be said that although the state has central control over immigration policy, exercising that power often begins with a limited contest between the state and interested social forces: agribusiness, manufacturing, humanitarian groups, unions, ethnic organizations, and zero-population-growth efforts, to name a few.[34] Today the old hierarchies of power and influence within the state are being reconfigured by increasing economic globalization and the ascendance of an international human rights regime.[35]

1. The State and the New Geography of Power

1. Reisman 1990, 867.

2. Franck 1992; Jacobson 1996.

3. Reisman 1990; McDougal and Reisman 1981.

4. Reisman 1990, 868.

5. See the classification of different types of relationships between a system of rule and territoriality in Ruggie 1993.

6. See Anderson 1974; Wallerstein 1974; Giddens 1985.

7. See Tilly 1990. On the Italian city-states and the Hanseatic League in northern Europe, see the analysis in Spruyt 1994.

8. See Mattingly's (1988) account of the right of embassy in medieval times as a specific, formal right with only partial immunities.

9. Mattingly 1988, 244. See also Kratochwil 1986.

10. In this case, the site for extraterritoriality is the individual holding diplomatic status.

11. Grotius's doctrine was a response to the Dutch East Indies Company's effort to monopolize access to the oceans; it resolved the vacuum left by the failure of Spain and Portugal to agree on a division of the maritime trade routes.

12. There is a vast literature on this subject. See, e.g., Bonacich et al. 1994; Morales 1994; Ward 1990.

13. See United Nations Centre for Transnational Corporations (UNCTAD) 1993, 1995. The center was an autonomous entity until 1994, when it became part of UNCTAD.

14. I elaborated these issues in Sassen 1991. This process of corporate integration should not be confused with vertical integration as conventionally defined. See also Gereffi and Korzeniewicz 1994 on commodity chains and Porter's (1990) value-added chains, two constructs that also illustrate the difference between corporate integration on a world scale and vertical integration as conventionally defined.

15. More detailed accounts of these figures and sources can be found in Sassen 1994a.

16. See, e.g., Harrison 1994.

17. See Sassen 1991, 1994a; Knox and Taylor 1995; Brotchie et al. 1995; *Le Débat*, 1994.

18. It is important to unbundle analytically the fact of strategic functions for the global economy or for global operation from the overall corporate economy of a country. Traditional economic complexes have valorization dynamics that tend to be far more articulated with the public economic functions of the state, the quintessential example being Fordist manufacturing. Global markets in finance and advanced services, however, partly operate under a regulatory umbrella that is market centered. This raises questions of control,

especially in view of the currently inadequate capacities to govern transactions in electronic space. Global control and command functions are partly handled within national corporate structures but also constitute a distinct corporate subsector, which can be conceived of as part of a network that connects global cities across the globe. In this sense, global cities are different from the old capitals of erstwhile empires, in that they are a function of cross-border networks rather than simply the most powerful city of an empire. There is, in my conceptualization, no such entity as a single global city akin to the single capital of an empire; the category "global city" only makes sense as a component of a global network of strategic sites. See Sassen 1991. For the purposes of certain kinds of inquiry, this distinction may not matter; for the purposes of understanding the global economy, it does.

19. These data come from the Bank for International Settlements, the so-called central bankers' bank.

20. See Mittelman 1996; Panitch 1996; Cox 1987.

21. There are, of course, other mechanisms for resolving business disputes. The larger system includes arbitration controlled by courts, arbitration that is parallel to courts, and various court and out-of-court mechanisms such as mediation. The following description of international commercial arbitration is taken from Dezalay and Garth 1995. For these authors, international commercial arbitration means something different today from what it did twenty years ago. Increasingly formal, it has come to resemble U.S.-style litigation as it has become more successful and institutionalized. Today, international business contracts for the sale of goods, joint ventures, construction projects, distributorships, and the like typically call for arbitration in the event of a dispute arising from the contractual arrangement. The main reason given for this choice is that arbitration allows each party to avoid being forced to submit to the courts of the other.

Also important is the secrecy of the process. Such arbitration can be institutional, following the rules of institutions such as the International Chamber of Commerce in Paris, the American Arbitration Association, the London Court of International Commercial Arbitration, or many others, or it can be ad hoc, often following the rules of the UN Commission on International Trade Law (UNCITRAL). The arbitrators, usually three private individuals selected by the parties, act as private judges, holding hearings and issuing judgments. There are few grounds for appeal to courts, and the final decision of the arbitrators is more easily enforced among signatory countries than would be a court judgment (under the terms of a widely adopted 1958 New York Convention).

22. Dezalay and Garth 1995; Aksen, 1990. Despite this increase in size, there is a kind of international arbitration community, a club of sorts, with relatively few important institutions and limited numbers of individuals in each country who are the key players both as counsel and arbitrators. But the enormous growth of arbitration over the last decade has led to sharp competition in the business; indeed, it has become big legal business (Salacuse 1991). Dezalay and Garth found that multinational legal firms sharpen the competition further because they have the capacity to forum shop among institutions, sets of rules, laws, and arbitrators. The large English and U.S. law firms have used their power in the international business world to impose their conception of arbitration and more largely of the practice of law. This is well illustrated by the case of France. Although French firms rank among the top providers of information services and industrial engineering services in Europe and have a strong though not outstanding position in financial and insurance services, they are at an increasing disadvantage in legal and accounting services. French law firms are at a particular disadvantage because of their legal system (the Napoleon-

ic Code): Anglo-American law tends to govern international transactions. Foreign firms with offices in Paris dominate the servicing of
the legal needs of firms in France, both French and foreign, that operate internationally (Carrez 1991) (see *Le Débat* 1994).

23. Summarized in Dezalay and Garth 1995; see also Dezalay 1992.

24. Dezalay and Garth 1995. The so-called lex mercatoria was
conceived by many as a return to an international law of business
independent of national laws (Carbonneau 1990). Anglo-American
practitioners tend not to support this Continental, highly academic
notion (see Carbonneau 1990), and insofar as they are "American-
izing" the field, they are moving it farther away from academic law
and lex mercatoria.

25. There are several rating agencies in other countries, but they
are oriented to the domestic markets. The possibility of a European-
based rating agency has been discussed, particularly with the merger
of a London-based agency (IBCA) with a French one (Euronotation).

26. As the demand for ratings grows, so does the authoritativeness
of the notion behind them. Sinclair (1994) considers this to be ill
founded given the judgments that are central to it. The processes
intrinsic to ratings are tied to certain assumptions, which are in turn
tied to dominant interests, notably narrow theories of market effi-
ciency. They aim for undistorted price signals and little if any government intervention. Sinclair notes that transition costs such as
unemployment are usually not factored into evaluations and considered to be outweighed by the new environment created (143).

27. Their power has grown in good part because of disintermediation and the globalization of the capital market. Some functions ful-
filled by banks (i.e., intermediation) have lost considerable weight in
the running of capital markets. Thus, insofar as banks are subject to
considerable government regulation and their successors are not,

government regulation over the capital markets has declined. Ratings agencies, which are private entities, have taken over some of the functions of banks in organizing information for suppliers and borrowers of capital. An important question is whether the new agencies and the larger complex of entities represented by Wall Street have indeed formed a new intermediary sector (see Thrift 1987).

28. Rosenau and Czempiel 1992.

29. See Trubek et al. 1993.

30. This hegemony has not passed unnoticed and is engendering considerable debate. For instance, a familiar issue that is emerging as significant in view of the spread of Western legal concepts involves a critical examination of the philosophical premises of authorship and property that define the legal arena in the West (e.g., Coombe 1993.)

31. See Shapiro 1993. There have been a few particular common developments and many particular parallel developments in law across the world. Thus, as a concomitant of the globalization of markets and the organization of transnational corporations, there has been a move toward relatively uniform global contract and commercial law. This can be seen as a private lawmaking system wherein two or more parties create a set of rules to govern their future relations. Such a system of private lawmaking can exist transnationally even when there is no transnational court or sovereign to resolve disputes and secure enforcement. The case of international commercial arbitration discussed earlier illustrates this well. See also Shapiro 1979.

32. Charny 1991; Trachtman 1993. Two other categories that may also partly overlap with internationalization are important to distinguish, at least analytically: multilateralism and what Ruggie (1993) has called multiperspectival institutions.

33. See Sinclair 1994.

34. For a discussion of the concept of cultural globalization, see King 1991 and Robertson 1991, especially Robertson's notion of the world as a single place, what he calls the "global human condition." I would say that globalization is also a process that produces differentiation, but of a character very different from that associated with such differentiating notions as national character, national culture, and national society. For example, the corporate world today has a global geography, but it isn't everywhere in the world: in fact, it has highly defined and structured spaces; it is also increasingly sharply differentiated from noncorporate segments in the economies of the particular locations (such as New York City) or countries where it operates.

35. Shapiro 1993 finds that law and the political structures that produce and sustain it are far more national and far less international than are trade and politics as such (63). He argues that the U.S. domestic legal regime may have to respond to global changes in markets and politics far more often than to global changes in law. For the most part, he claims, national regimes of law and lawyering will remain self-generating, though in response to globally perceived needs. In my reading, it is this last point that may well be emerging as a growing factor in shaping legal form and legal practice.

36. The best-known instance of this is probably the austerity policy imposed on many developing countries. Such policies also point up the participation of states in furthering the goals of globalization, because they have to be run through national governments and reprocessed as national policies. It is clearer here than in other cases that the global is not simply the non-national, that global processes materialize in national territories and institutions. There is a distinction here to be made—and to be specified theoretically and empirically—between international law (whether public or private), which is always implemented through national govern-

ments, and these policies, which are part of the effort to foster globalization.

37. Dezalay 1992. See also Carrez 1991; and Sinclair 1994.

38. Shapiro 1993.

39. Shapiro 1993, 39; Wiegand 1991.

40. Dezalay 1992.

41. Aman 1995, 437.

42. See Panitch 1996; Cox 1987; Mittelman 1996.

43. Aman, 1995; Young 1989; Rosenau 1992.

44. Ruggie 1993, 143.

45. See Kennedy 1988; Negri 1995.

2. On Economic Citizenship

1. See, e.g., Kalberg 1993; Seligman 1993; Turner 1990; Giddens 1985.

2. Otto Hintze further developed these ideas in his study of the origins of citizenship in feudalism, particularly the notions of immunity emerging in that period. See Gilbert 1975.

3. Franck 1992 examines how representative democracy has become a condition for legitimating governments.

4. See, for instance, the analysis in Kalberg 1993 showing the extent to which a certain combination of conditions had to be secured for the institution of modern citizenship to emerge. Using a rather confined definition, the author succeeds brilliantly in demonstrating the rarity of this combination of conditions.

5. See, for example, the new scholarship on the possibility of the erosion of citizenship as an institution embedded in nation-states, notably the work by Baubock 1994 and Soysal 1994.

6. See, for example, Kalberg 1993; Hindess 1993.

7. See Soysal 1994 for an analysis of the limits of citizenship in Europe today.

8. See, for example, Baubock 1994, which asks whether human rights can be "usefully understood as universalized rights of citizenship that are extended to a transnational level" (239). See also Roche 1992; Smith 1990.

9. See, for instance, the well-known argument that "freedom, wherever it existed as a tangible reality, has always been spatially limited" (see Arendt 1963, 279). See Walzer 1983 on the relation between closed states and substantive freedom and justice. See Holston 1996 on cities and citizenship today.

10. See, for instance, Holston 1996; Basch, Schiller, and Szanton-Blanc 1994.

11. Economic citizenship is not part of the conventionally understood history and theory of citizenship, but it can be said that there is no theory as such of citizenship, only typologies and histories of the institution.

12. See Marshall 1977, 1981. Marshall's work on citizenship addresses the tension between political democracy and the condition of class inequality; he sees the welfare state as contributing to reduce the tension. This work has generated a large literature; it is impossible to do justice to it here.

13. See, for instance, Collins et al. 1993. See Newman 1988 on inequality.

14. Woodall 1995, b.

15. Ibid., 11–12.

16. Ibid.

17. McKinsey Global Institute 1994, qtd. in Woodall 1995. The potential for further growth is illustrated, for example, by the case of the Russian stock market. Both India and Russia have recently opened

their markets to foreign investors. Many Russian firms, however, are very reluctant to list their stock publicly, so turnover in the Russian stock market is dominated by over-the-counter trading in about a hundred stocks, with a turnover of at most 50 million dollars a week. In Bombay, by contrast, the average weekly turnover is 290 million dollars. Clearly, Russia represents an enormous potential for growth in terms of equity trading.

18. For instance, figures show that countries with high savings have high domestic investment. In other words, most savings are still invested in the domestic economy. Only 10 percent of the assets of the world's five hundred largest institutional portfolios are invested in foreign assets (see Woodall 1995, 8). Some argue that a more integrated capital market would raise this level significantly and hence increase individual nations' vulnerability to and dependence on the capital markets. It should be noted that extrapolating the potential for growth from the current level of 10 percent may be somewhat dubious, in that such projections may not reflect the full range of factors that keep managers from using the option of cross-border investments. Cross-border investment may well remain underused regardless of the actual potentials of the system.

19. There was an international financial market in late medieval Europe, of course. For some scholars, these are just two phases in a long history. See, for example, Braudel's (1982) notion of financial expansions as closing phases of major capitalist developments, and Arrighi's (1994) examination of the Genoese and Dutch periods of international financial domination as part of his explanation of the global capital market today. These scholars reject the notion that there was a new stage of capitalism in the form of finance capital at the end of the nineteenth century (see Hilferding 1981). Nor do they believe that there was a "cosmopolitan network of high finance . . . as

peculiar to the last third of the nineteenth century and the first third of the twentieth century as Polanyi thought. Its similarities with the cosmopolitan network that had regulated the European monetary system three centuries earlier during the Age of the Genoese are quite striking" (Arrighi 1994, 167).

20. On this point, see Susan Strange's account of the current situation in *Casino Capitalism* (1986); see also Sassen 1991, part 1.

21. For many analysts, the anomaly is the period from 1930 to 1970, a period when tight capital controls and regulations protected domestic financial markets and gave governments more control over their economies. There were always leaks, and they grew sharply in the 1960s. One response to tight controls at home was the implementation of the market in Eurodollars, which was developed by U.S. banks to escape banking regulations at home. Then the collapse of key elements of the Bretton Woods system in the early 1970s marked a new emergence of the global capital market.

22. See ibid., 5. In addition, much of the evidence and literature on which this and the next section are based can be found in Sassen 1991 and forthcoming.

23. Woodall 1995, 11.

24. We now also know that the particular organizational structure of savings-and-loans associations made possible unusually high levels of fraud and that this was a major factor contributing to their financial crisis. We also know from historians on the subject that the possibilities for fraud have long been high in these types of organizations.

25. Woodall 1995, 1b.

26. Since these derivatives entail a redistribution of interest sensitivities from one firm or sector to another, one could argue that the overall sensitivity to interest rates in the economy remains constant. But the fact is that different firms may have different sensitivities to

changes in interest rates; apparently, highly sensitive firms are shifting their risk to less sensitive firms, which reduces the overall impact of interest rates on the economy.

27. See, for instance, Arrighi 1994.

28. See some of the work by David Kennedy, e.g., Kennedy 1988; 1995.

29. See Panitch 1996; Mittelman 1996; Sassen forthcoming.

30. See Duncan Kennedy 1993, especially the argument that in the case of the United States these ground rules contain rules of permission that strengthen the power of employers over workers or allow an unnecessary concentration of wealth in the name of the protection of property rights.

31. The term GATT-MTN (Multilateral Trade Negotiations) refers to the increasingly complex body of agreements, institutions, and procedures created and administered under the general aegis of the GATT. The primary elements of the system are the GATT itself and the agreements on nontariff measures produced by the Tokyo Round of multilateral trade negotiations and the Uruguay Round. As the system develops, its central institutions become increasingly complex. Implementing the Uruguay Round, the largest and most complex in the history of the GATT, will require greater institutional development. The WTO is one such development; many others will arise as the system evolves and is implemented. See Jackson 1989; Bhagwati 1991.

32. For instance, the private interests argument provides a strong and consistent rationale for many of the dispute settlement reforms developed during the Uruguay Round. See Abbott 1992.

33. See Ruggie's work (1996) on multilateral agreements.

34. See Aman 1995.

35. See Franck 1992.

3. Immigration Tests the New Order

1. A vast and rich scholarly literature documents and interprets the specificity and distinctiveness of immigration policy in highly developed countries; see, e.g., Weil 1991; Cornelius, Martin, and Hollifield 1994; Weiner 1995; Soysal 1994; Thranhardt 1992; Bade 1992—to mention just a few. As a body, this literature reveals the many differences among these countries.

2. Refugee policy in some countries does lift the burden of immigration from the immigrant's shoulders. U.S. policy, for example, particularly for Indochinese refugees, acknowledges partial responsibility on the part of the government. Clearly, in the case of economic migration, such responsibility is far more difficult to establish and by its nature is far more indirect.

3. I should note that the right to entry is part of the 1969 Convention on Refugee Problems in Africa adopted by the Organization of African States.

4. Plender 1988, 159–91.

5. For instance, major human rights codes place procedural restrictions on lawful expulsions; bilateral and regional accords for employment migration tend to contain provisions through which member states relinquish some control over the entry and exit of foreigners. See Plender 1988; Goodwin-Gill 1988.

6. See, e.g., Hollifield 1992; Baubock 1994; Sassen forthcoming.

7. The efforts that mix the conventions on universal human rights and national judiciaries assume many different forms. Some examples in the United States are the sanctuary movement in the 1980s, which sought to establish protected areas, typically in churches, for refugees from Central America; judicial battles such as those around the status of Salvadorans granted indefinite stays though formally defined as

illegal; and the fight for the rights of detained Haitians in an earlier wave of boat lifts. It is clear in these cases that notwithstanding the lack of an enforcement apparatus, human rights limit the discretion of states in how they treat non-nationals on their territory. It is also worth noting in this regard that the United Nations High Commissioner for Refugees (UNHCR) is the only UN agency with the authority to intercede worldwide on behalf of those in danger.

8. While these developments are well known in Europe and North America, there is not much general awareness that incipient forms are showing up in Japan as well (see, e.g., Sassen 1991, chap. 9; Shank 1994). For instance, in Japan today a strong group of human rights advocates is working on behalf of immigrants; nonofficial unions are trying to organize undocumented immigrant workers; and organizations working on behalf of immigrants are receiving funding from individuals or government institutions in sending countries (e.g., the Thai ambassador to Japan announced in October 1995 that his government will give a total of 2.5 million baht, about 100,000 U.S. dollars, to five civic groups that assist Thai migrant workers, especially undocumented ones; see *Japan Times*, October 18, 1995; see also Sassen 1993).

9. Further, the growth of immigration, refugee flows, ethnicity, and regionalism challenges the accepted notion of citizenship in contemporary nation-states and hence the formal structures for accountability. My research on the international circulation of capital and labor caused me to review the meaning of such concepts as national economy and national workforce under conditions of growing internationalization of capital in both developed and developing countries and the burgeoning presence of immigrant workers in major industrial countries. Furthermore, the rise of ethnicity in the United States and Europe among a mobile workforce raises questions about the

content of the concept of nation-based citizenship. The portability of national identity gives rise to concerns about bonds with other countries, or localities within them, and the resurgence of ethnic regionalism creates barriers to the political incorporation of new immigrants. See, e.g., Soysal 1994; Baubock 1994; Sassen forthcoming).

10. There is a large and rich literature on the development of immigration policy at the European level; please refer to n. 1, above, for a few citations. Longer bibliographies and analyses of the particular angle under discussion here—limitations on the autonomy of the state in making immigration policy—can also be found in Sassen forthcoming.

11. Mitchell 1989.

12. Diverse social forces shape the role of the state depending on the matter at hand. Thus in the early 1980s bank crisis, for instance, the players were few and well coordinated; the state basically relinquished the organizing capacity to the banks, the IMF, and a few other actors. It was all very discreet—indeed, so discreet that the government was hardly a player in the crisis. This is quite a contrast with the deliberations around the passing of the 1986 Immigration and Reform Control Act, which was a national brawl. In trade liberalization discussions, too, there are often multiple players, and the executive may or may not relinquish powers to congress.

13. Aman (1995) has noted that although political and constitutional arguments for reallocating federal power to the states are not new, the recent reemergence of the Tenth Amendment as a politically viable and popular guideline is a major political shift in the relations between the federal government and the states since the New Deal.

14. Reimers 1983; Briggs 1992.

15. Sassen 1988, 1993; *Journal fur Entwicklungspolitik* 1995; Bonacich et al. 1994.

16. Mahler 1995.

17. Sassen forthcoming.

18. For a more detailed account, see Sassen 1993; Shank 1994.

19. See Sassen 1993.

20. E.g., Cornelius, Martin, and Hollifield 1994.

21. Bosniak 1992, 745.

22. Sassen 1993.

23. Jacobson 1996; Reisman 1990.

24. Henkin 1990, 144.

25. It is interesting to note that in the International Court of Justice it is very rare for a judge to vote against the position of his or her government in disputes before the court. This is not at all uncommon, however, in the European Court of Human Rights; indeed, it is becoming more common. This is significant because the European Court has become the main organ for the interpretation of the European human rights convention's provisions.

26. For instance, the Universal Declaration was cited in 76 federal cases from 1948 through 1994; over 90 percent of those cases took place after 1980, and, of those, 49 percent involved immigration issues, a proportion that rises to 54 percent if cases involving refugees are included (Jacobson 1996, 97). Jacobson also found that the term *human rights* was cited in 19 federal cases before the twentieth century, in 34 from 1900 to 1944, in 191 from 1945 to 1969, in 803 in the 1970s, and in more than 2,000 in the 1980s. He estimates that such references will have been made in more than 4,000 cases by the end of the 1990s.

27. See, e.g., Hassan 1983.

28. Jacobson 1996, 100.

29. See Shapiro 1991.

30. See Bosniak 1992 for an in-depth examination of this convention and its potentials and limitations for the protection of undocumented migrants.

31. It is perhaps worth noting that after much debate, undocumented migrants were also included under the protections provided by the UN General Assembly's 1985 Declaration on the Human Rights of Individuals Who Are Not Citizens of the Countries in Which They Live. But being a nonbinding instrument it is probably of little use to undocumented migrants.

32. See, e.g., Jacobson 1996; Soysal 1994.

33. Jacobson 1996.

34. Cf. Mitchell 1989.

35. An example is the ascendance of so-called soft security issues: according to some observers, recent government reorganization in the State Department, the Department of Defense, and the CIA reflects an implicit redefinition of national security.

BIBLIOGRAPHY

Abbott, Kenneth W. 1992. "GATT as a Public Institution: The Uruguay Round and Beyond." *Brooklyn Journal of International Law* 18, no. 1: 31–85.

Abu-Lughod, Janet. 1989. *Before European Hegemony: The World System A.D. 1250–1350.* New York: Oxford University Press.

Abu-Lughod, Janet Lippman. 1995. "Comparing Chicago, New York, and Los Angeles: Testing Some World Cities Hypotheses." In Paul L. Knox and Peter J. Taylor, eds., *World Cities in a World-System*, pp. 171–91. Cambridge: Cambridge University Press.

Aglietta, Michel, and André Orléan. 1982. *La violence de la monnaie.* Paris: Presses Universitaires de France.

Aksen, Gerald. 1990. "Arbitration and Other Means of Dispute Settlement." In D. Goldsweig and R. Cummings, eds., *Inter-*

national Joint Ventures: A Practical Approach to Working with Foreign Investors in the U.S. and Abroad, pp. 287–94. Chicago: American Bar Association.

Aman, Alfred C., Jr. 1995. "A Global Perspective on Current Regulatory Reform: Rejection, Relocation, or Reinvention? *Indiana Journal of Global Legal Studies* 2:429–64.

Amin, A., and Thrift, N. 1992. "Neo-Marshallian Nodes in Global Networks." *International Journal of Urban and Regional Research* 16, no. 4: 571–87.

Anderson, Perry. 1974. *Lineages of the Absolutist State*. London: New Left Books.

Arena, Luis C., ed. 1995. *Globalization, Integration and Human Rights in the Caribbean*. Bogotá, Colombia: Instituto Latinoamericano de Servicios Legales (ILSA).

Arendt, Hannah. 1963. *On Revolution*. London: Faber and Faber.

Arrighi, Giovanni. 1994. *The Long Twentieth Century: Money, Power, and the Origins of Our Times*. London: Verso.

Atik, Jeffery. 1994. "Fairness and Managed Foreign Direct Investment." *Columbia Journal of Transnational Law* 32, no. 1: 1–42.

Bade, Klaus J., ed. 1992. *Deutsche im Ausland, Fremde in Deutschland: Migration in Geschichte und Gegenwart*. Munich: C. H. Beck.

Balibar, Etienne. 1990. "The Nation Form: History and Ideology." *Review* 13, no. 3: 329–61.

Basch, Linda, Nina Glick Schiller, and Cristina Szanton-Blanc. 1994. *Nations Unbound: Transnational Projects, Postcolonial Predicaments and Deterritorialized Nation-States*. Amsterdam: Gordon and Breach.

Baubock, Rainer. 1994. *Transnational Citizenship: Membership and Rights in International Migration*. Aldershot, England: Edward Elgar.

Berman, Nathaniel. 1995. "Economic Consequences, Nationalist Passions: Keynes, Crisis, Culture, and Policy." *American University Journal of International Law and Policy* (special issue) 10, no. 2 (winter): 619–70.

Bhagwati, Jagdish. 1991. *The World Trading System at Risk*. Princeton: Princeton University Press.

Body-Gendrot, S. 1993. *Ville et violence*. Paris: Presses Universitaires de France.

Bohning, W. R., and M.-L. Schloeter-Paredes, eds. 1994. *Aid in Place of Migration*. Geneva: International Labor Office.

Bonacich, Edna, Lucie Cheng, Norma Chinchilla, Nora Hamilton, and Paul Ong, eds. 1994. *Global Production: The Apparel Industry in the Pacific Rim*. Philadelphia: Temple University Press.

Bose, Christine E., and Edna Acosta-Belen, eds. 1995. *Women in the Latin American Development Process*. Philadelphia: Temple University Press.

Bosniak, Linda S. 1994. "Membership, Equality, and the Difference that Alienage Makes." *New York University Law Review* 69: 1047–1149.

———. 1992. "Human Rights, State Sovereignty and the Protection of Undocumented Migrants Under the International Migrant Workers Convention." *International Migration Review* 25, no. 4: 737–70.

Braudel, Fernand. 1982. *The Wheels of Commerce*. New York: Harper and Row.

Briggs, Vernon M., Jr. 1992. *Mass Immigration and the National Interest*. Armonk, N.Y.: M. E. Sharpe.

Brotchie, John, Mike Batty, Ed Blakely, Peter Hall, and Peter Newton, eds. 1995. *Cities in Competition: Productive and Sustainable Cities for the Twenty-first Century*. Melbourne: Longman Australia.

Carbonneau, Thomas, ed. 1990. *Lex Mercatoria and Arbitration.* Dobbs Ferry, N.Y.: Transnational Juris Publications.

Carrez, Jean-François. 1991. *Le développement des fonctions tertiares internationales à Paris et dans les métropoles régionales: Rapport au premier ministre.* Paris: La Documentation française.

Castells, Manuel. 1989. *The Informational City.* Oxford: Blackwell.

Charny, David. 1991. "Competition among Jurisdictions in Formulating Corporate Law Rules: An American Perspective on the 'Race to the Bottom' in the European Communities." *Harvard International Law Journal* 32, no. 2: 423–56.

Collins, Sheila D., Helen Lachs Ginsburg, and Gertrude Schaffner Goldberg, in consultation with Ward Morehouse, Leonard Rodberg, Sumner Rosen, and June Zaccone. 1994. *Jobs for All: A Plan for the Revitalization of America.* New York: New Initiatives for Full Employment.

Compa, Lance. 1993. "International Labor Rights and the Sovereignty Question: NAFTA and Guatemala, Two Case Studies." *American University Journal of International Law and Policy* 9, no. 1 (fall): 117–50.

Competition and Change: Journal of Global Business and Political Economy. 1995. Vol. 1, no. 1.

Coombe, Rosemary J. 1993. "The Properties of Culture and the Politics of Possessing Identity: Native Claims in the Cultural Appropriation Controversy." *Canadian Journal of Law and Jurisprudence* 6, no. 2 (July): 249–85.

Cornelius, Wayne A., Philip L. Martin, and James F. Hollifield, eds. 1994. *Controlling Immigration: A Global Perspective.* Stanford, Calif.: Stanford University Press.

Cox, Robert. 1987. *Production, Power, and World Order: Social Forces in the Making of History.* New York: Columbia University Press.

Le Débat. 1994. *Le Nouveau Paris* (special issue) (summer).

Dezalay, Yves. 1992. *Marchands de droit.* Paris: Fayard.

Dezalay, Yves, and Bryant Garth. 1995. "Merchants of Law as Moral Entrepreneurs: Constructing International Justice from the Competition for Transnational Business Disputes." *Law and Society Review* 29, no. 1: 27–64.

Drache, D., and M. Gertler, eds. 1991. *The New Era of Global Competition: State Policy and Market Power.* Montreal: McGill-Queen's University Press.

Fainstein, Susan. 1993. *The City Builders.* Oxford: Blackwell.

Falk, R. A., and W. F. Henreider, eds. 1968. *International Law and Organization.* Philadelphia: Lippincott.

Fassman, Heinz, and Rainer Münz. *European Migration in the Late Twentieth Century: Historical Patterns, Actual Trends, and Social Implications.* Aldershot and Brookfield, England: Edward Elgar.

Franck, Thomas M. 1992. "The Emerging Right to Democratic Governance." *American Journal of International Law* 86, no. 1: 46–91.

Gereffi, Gary, and Miguel Korzeniewicz, eds. 1994. *Commodity Chains and Global Capitalism.* Westport, Conn.: Praeger.

Giddens, Anthony. 1987. *The Nation-State and Violence.* Berkeley: University of California Press.

Gilbert, Felix. 1975. *The Historical Essays of Otto Hintze.* New York: Oxford University Press.

Gill, Stephen, ed. 1993. *Gramsci, Historical Materialism and International Relations.* Cambridge: Cambridge University Press.

Glickman, N. J., and A. K. Glasmeier. 1989. "The International Economy and the American South." In L. Rodwin and H. Sazanami, eds., *Deindustrialization and Regional Economic Transformation: The Experience of the United States.* Winchester, Mass.: Unwin Hyman.

Global Crisis, Local Struggles. 1993. *Social Justice* (special issue) 20, nos. 3–4 (fall–winter).

Goldstein, Judith, and Robert O. Keohane, eds. 1993. *Ideas and Foreign Policy: Beliefs, Institutions, and Political Change*. Ithaca, N.Y.: Cornell University Press.

Goodwin-Gill, G. S. 1989. "Nonrefoulement and the New Asylum Seekers." In D. A. Martin, ed., *The New Asylum Seekers: Refugee Policy in the 1980s*. Dordrecht, the Netherlands: Martinus Nijhoff.

Habermas, Jurgen. 1992. "Citizenship and National Identity: Some Reflections on the Future of Europe." *Praxis International* 12, no. 1: 1–19.

Harrison, Bennett. 1994. *Lean and Mean: The Changing Landscape of Corporate Power in the Age of Flexibility*. New York: Basic Books.

Harvey, David. 1989. *The Urban Experience*. Oxford: Blackwell.

Hassan, Farooq. 1983. "The Doctrine of Incorporation." *Human Rights Quarterly* 5:68–86.

Haus, Leah. 1995. "Openings in the Wall: Transnational Migrants, Labor Unions, and U.S. Immigration Policy." *International Organization* 49, no. 2 (spring): 285–313.

Heisler, Martin. 1986. "Transnational Migration as a Small Window on the Diminished Autonomy of the Modern Democratic State." *Annals (American Academy of Political and Social Science)* 485 (May): 153–66.

Henderson, Jeffrey. 1989. *The Globalization of High Technology Production: Society, Space, and Semiconductors in the Restructuring of the Modern World*. New York: Routledge.

Henkin, Louis. 1990. *The Age of Rights*. New York: Columbia University Press.

Hilferding, Rudolf. 1981. *Finance Capital: A Study of the Latest Phase of Capitalist Development*. London: Routledge and Kegan Paul.

Hindess, Barry. 1993. "Citizenship in the Modern West." In Bryan S. Turner, ed., *Citizenship and Social Theory*, pp. 19–35. London: Sage Publications.

Hobsbawm, Eric. 1991. *Nations and Nationalism Since 1780: Programme, Myth, Reality*. Cambridge: Cambridge University Press.

Hollifield, James F. 1992. *Immigrants, Markets, and States*. Cambridge: Harvard University Press.

Holston, James, ed. 1996. *Cities and Citizenship. Public Culture* (special issue) 8, no. 2 (winter).

Hopkins, Terence K. 1990. "Notes on the Concept of Hegemony." *Review* 13, no. 3: 409–11.

Hugo, Graeme. 1995. "Indonesia's Migration Transition." *Journal für Entwicklungspolitik* 11, no. 3: 285–309.

Hymer, Stephen, and Robert Rowthorn. 1970. "Multinational Corporations and International Oligopoly." In Charles P. Kindleberger, ed., *The International Corporation*, pp. 57–91. Cambridge, Mass.: MIT Press.

Ibister, John. 1995. *The Immigration Debate: Remaking America*. West Hartford, Conn.: Kumarian.

Jackson, John H. 1989. *The World Trading System: Law and Policy of International Economic Relations*. Cambridge: MIT Press.

Jacobson, David. 1996. *Rights Across Borders: Immigration and the Decline of Citizenship*. Baltimore: Johns Hopkins University Press.

Jessop, Robert. 1990. *State Theory: Putting Capitalist States in Their Place*. University Park: Pennsylvania State University Press.

Kahler, Miles, ed. 1986. *The Politics of International Debt*. Ithaca, N.Y.: Cornell University Press.

Kalberg, Stephen. 1993. "Cultural Foundations of Modern Citizenship." In Bryan S. Turner, ed., *Citizenship and Social Theory*, pp. 91–114. London: Sage Publications.

Katzenstein, Peter. 1985. *Small States in World Markets: Industrial Policy in Europe*. Ithaca, N.Y.: Cornell University Press.

Kennedy, David. 1995. "The International Style in Postwar Law and Policy: John Jackson and the Field of International Economic Law." *American University Journal of International Law and Policy* (special issue) 10, no. 2 (winter): 671–716.

———. 1988. "A New Stream of International Law Scholarship." *Wisconsin International Law Journal* 7, no. 1: 1–49.

Kennedy, Duncan. 1993. "The Stakes of Law, or Hale and Foucault!" In *Sexy Dressing Etc.: Essays on the Power and Politics of Cultural Identity*, pp. 83–125. Cambridge: Harvard University Press.

Keohane, Robert. 1984. *After Hegemony: Cooperation and Discord in the World Political Economy*. Princeton, N.J.: Princeton University Press.

King, Anthony D., ed. 1991. *Culture, Globalization, and the World-System: Contemporary Conditions for the Representation of Identity*. Current Debates in Art History 3. Binghamton: Department of Art and Art History, State University of New York at Binghamton.

Knox, Paul L., and Peter J. Taylor, eds. 1995. *World Cities in a World-System*. Cambridge: Cambridge University Press.

Kooiman, Jan, and Martin van Vliet. 1993. "Governance and Public Management." In K. A. Eliassen and J. Kooiman, eds., *Managing Public Organizations: Lessons from Contemporary European Experience*, pp. 58–72. London: Sage Publications.

Krasner, Stephen. 1979. "The Tokyo Round: Particularistic Interests and Prospects for Stability in the Global Trading System." *International Studies Quarterly* 23, no. 4: 491–531.

Kratochwil, Friedrich. 1986. "Of Systems, Boundaries and Territoriality." *World Politics* 34 (October): 27–52.

Lash, Scott, and John Urry. 1987. *The End of Organized Capitalism*. Madison: University of Wisconsin Press.

Lefort, C. 1988. *Democracy and Political Theory*. Cambridge: Polity.

McDougal, M. S., and W. M. Reisman. 1981. *International Law Essays: A Supplement to International Law in Contemporary Perspective*. Mineola, N.Y.: Foundation Press.

Mahler, Sarah. 1995. *American Dreaming: Immigrant Life on the Margins*. Princeton, N.J.: Princeton University Press.

Marshall, T. H. 1981. *The Right to Welfare and Other Essays*. London: Heinemann.

———. 1977. *Class, Citizenship, and Social Development*. Chicago and London: University of Chicago Press.

Massey, Douglas S., Joaquin Arango, Graeme Hugo, Ali Kouaouci, Adela Pellegrino, and J. Edward Taylor. 1993. "Theories of International Migration: A Review and Appraisal." *Population and Development Review* 19, no. 3: 431–66.

Mattingly, Garrett. 1988. *Renaissance Diplomacy*. New York: Dover.

Mazlish, Bruce, and Ralph Buultjens, eds. 1993. *Conceptualizing Global History*. Boulder, Colo.: Westview.

Mitchell, Christopher. 1989. "International Migration, International Relations, and Foreign Policy." *International Migration Review* 3, no. 3 (fall): 681–708.

Mittelman, James H., ed. 1996. *Globalization: Critical Reflections. International Political Economy Yearbook*, vol. 9. Boulder, Colo.: Lynne Riener.

Modelski, George, and Susan Modelski, eds. 1988. *Documenting Global Leadership*. Seattle: University of Washington Press.

Morales, Rebecca. *Flexible Production: Restructuring of the International Automobile Industry*. Cambridge: Polity.

Negri, Toni. 1995. "A quoi sert encore l'Etat?" *Pouvoirs Pouvoir. Futur Antérieur* (special issue) 25–26: 135–52.

Nye, Joseph S., Jr. 1990. *Bound to Lead: The Changing Nature of American Power*. New York: Basic.

Offe, Claus. 1985. *Disorganized Capitalism: Contemporary Transformations of Work and Politics*. Cambridge, Mass.: MIT Press.

Panitch, Leo. 1996. "Rethinking the Role of the State in an Era of Globalization." In James H. Mittelman, ed., *Globalization: Critical Reflections, International Political Economy Yearbook*, vol. 9. Boulder, Colo.: Lynne Riener.

Paul, Joel R. 1994–95. "Free Trade, Regulatory Competition, and the Autonomous Market Fallacy." *Columbia Journal of European Law* 1, no. 1 (fall/winter): 29–62.

——, ed. 1995. *Interdisciplinary Approaches to International Economic Law. American University Journal of International Law and Policy* (special issue) 10, no. 2 (winter).

Plender, R. 1988. *International Migration Law*. Dordrecht, the Netherlands: Martinus Nijhoff.

Porter, Michael E. 1990. *The Competitive Advantage of Nations*. New York: Free Press.

Reich, Robert. 1992. *The Work of Nations: Preparing Ourselves for Twenty-first Century Capitalism*. New York: Random House.

Reimers, David M. 1983. "An Unintended Reform: The 1965 Immigration Act and Third World Immigration to the U.S." *Journal of American Ethnic History* 3 (fall): 9–28.

Reisman, W. Michael. 1990. "Sovereignty and Human Rights in Contemporary International Law." *American Journal of International Law* 84, no. 4 (October): 866–76.

Robertson, R. 1991. "Social Theory, Cultural Relativity, and the Problem of Globality." In Anthony D. King, ed., *Culture, Globalization, and the World-System: Contemporary Conditions for the Representation of Identity*, pp. 69–90. Current Debates in Art History 3. Binghamton: Department of Art and Art History, State University of New York at Binghamton.

Roche, Maurice. 1992. *Rethinking Citizenship*. Cambridge: Polity.

Roepke, Wilhelm. 1954. "Economic Order and International Law." *Recueil des Cours* 86, no. 2: 203–50.

Rosen, Fred, and Deirdre McFadyen, eds. 1995. *Free Trade and Economic Restructuring in Latin America*. A NACLA Reader. New York: Monthly Review Press.

Rosenau, J. N. 1992. "Governance, Order, and Change in World Politics." In J. N. Rosenau and E. O. Czempiel, eds., *Governance Without Government: Order and Change in World Politics*, pp. 1–29. Cambridge: Cambridge University Press.

Rosenau, J. N., and E. O. Czempiel, eds. 1992. *Governance Without Government: Order and Change in World Politics*. Cambridge: Cambridge University Press.

Ross, Robert J. S., and Kent C. Trachte. 1990. *Global Capitalism: The New Leviathan*. Albany, N.Y.: SUNY Press.

Ruggie, John Gerard. 1993. "Territoriality and Beyond: Problematizing Modernity in International Relations." *International Organization* 47, no. 1 (winter): 139–74.

———. 1996. *Winning the Peace: America and World Order in the New Era*. New York: Columbia University Press.

Salacuse, Jeswald. 1991. *Making Global Deals: Negotiating in the International Marketplace*. Boston: Houghton Mifflin.

Sassen, Saskia. Forthcoming. *Immigration Policy in a Global Economy*. New York: Twentieth Century Fund.

——. 1996. *Immigrants and Refugees: A European Dilemma?* Frankfurt: Fischer.

——. 1994a. *Cities in a World Economy*. Thousand Oaks, Calif.: Pine Forge/Sage.

——. 1994b. "The Informal Economy: Between New Developments and Old Regulations." *Yale Law Journal* 103, no. 8 (June): 2289–2304.

——. 1993. "The Impact of Economic Internationalization on Immigration: Comparing the U.S. and Japan." *International Migration* 31, no. 1: 73–99.

——. 1991. *The Global City: New York, London, Tokyo*. Princeton, N.J.: Princeton University Press.

——. 1988. *The Mobility of Labor and Capital: A Study in International Investment and Labor Flow*. Cambridge: Cambridge University Press.

Schuck, Peter H., and Rogers M. Smith. 1985. *Citizenship Without Consent: Illegal Aliens in the American Polity*. New Haven: Yale University Press.

Schwerpunkt: Migration. 1995. *Journal für Entwicklungspolitik* (special issue on migration) 11, no. 3.

Seligman, Adam B. 1993. "The Fragile Ethical Vision of Civil Society." In Bryan S. Turner, ed., *Citizenship and Social Theory*, pp. 139–61. London: Sage.

Shank, G., ed. 1994. *Japan Enters the Twenty-first Century*. *Social Justice* (special issue) 21, no. 2 (summer).

Shapiro, Martin. 1993. "The Globalization of Law." *Indiana Journal of Global Legal Studies* 1 (fall): 37–64.

———. 1979. "Judicial Activism." In S. M. Lipset, ed., *The Third Century: America as a Post-industrial Society*. Stanford, Calif.: Hoover Institution Press–Stanford University.

Shelton, Dinah. 1991. "Representative Democracy and Human Rights in the Western Hemisphere." *Human Rights Law Journal* 12, no. 10 (October 31): 353–59.

Sikkink, Kathryn. 1993. "Human Rights, Principled Issue-Networks, and Sovereignty in Latin America." *International Organization* 47 (summer): 411–41.

Sinclair, Timothy J. 1994. "Passing Judgement: Credit Rating Processes as Regulatory Mechanisms of Governance in the Emerging World Order." *Review of International Political Economy* 1, no. 1 (spring): 133–59.

Smith, David A., and Michael Timberlake. 1995. "Cities in Global Matrices: Toward Mapping the World System's City System." In Paul L. Knox and Peter J. Taylor, eds., *World Cities in a World-System*, pp. 79–97. Cambridge: Cambridge University Press.

Smith, Dennis. 1990. *Capitalist Democracy on Trial: The Atlantic Debate from Tocqueville to the Present*. London: Routledge.

Soysal, Yasmin. 1994. *Limits of Citizenship*. Chicago: University of Chicago Press.

Spruyt, Hendrik. 1994. *The Sovereign State and Its Competitors: An Analysis of Systems Change*. Princeton, N.J.: Princeton University Press.

Steiner, Henry J. 1988. "Political Participation as a Human Right." *Harvard Human Rights Yearbook* 1 (spring): 77–134.

Storper, Michael, and Richard Walker. 1989. *The Capitalist*

Imperative: Territory, Technology, and Industrial Growth. Oxford: Blackwell.

Strange, Susan. 1986. *Casino Capitalism*. Oxford: Blackwell.

Sunstein, Cass R. "Incompletely Theorized Agreements." *Harvard Law Review* 108, no. 7 (May): 1733–72.

Taylor, Peter J. "World Cities and Territorial States: The Rise and Fall of Their Mutuality." In Paul L. Knox and Peter J. Taylor, eds., *World Cities in a World-System*, pp. 48–62. Cambridge: Cambridge University Press.

Thranhardt, Dietrich, ed. 1992. *Europe: A New Immigration Continent*. Hamburg: Lit.

Thrift, N. 1987. "The Fixers: The Urban Geography of International Commercial Capital." In J. Henderson and M. Castells, eds., *Global Restructuring and Territorial Development*. London: Sage.

Tilly, Charles. 1990. *Coercion, Capital, and European States, A.D. 990–1990*. Oxford: Blackwell.

——, ed. 1975. *The Formation of National States in Western Europe*. Princeton, N.J.: Princeton University Press.

Trachtman, Joel. 1993. "International Regulatory Competition, Externalization, and Jurisdiction." *Harvard International Law Journal* 34, no. 1: 47–104.

Trubek, David M., Yves Dezalay, Ruth Buchanan, and John R. Davis. 1993. "Global Restructuring and the Law: The Internationalization of Legal Fields and Creation of Transnational Arenas." Working Paper Series on the Political Economy of Legal Change. No. 1. Madison: Global Studies Research Program, University of Wisconsin.

Turner, Bryan S., ed. 1993. *Citizenship and Social Theory*. London: Sage.

———. 1990. "Outline of a Theory of Citizenship." *Sociology* 24, no. 2: 189–214.

United Nations, Centre for Transnational Corporations. 1992. *World Investment Report 1992: Transnational Corporations as Engines of Growth*. New York: United Nations, Centre for Transnational Corporations.

United Nations Conference on Trade and Development (UNCTAD). 1995. *1995 World Investment Report: Transnational Corporations and Competitiveness*. New York: UNCTAD, Division on Transnational Corporations and Investment.

———. 1993. *1993 World Investment Report: Transnational Corporations and Integrated International Production*. New York: UNCTAD, Programme on Transnational Corporations of the United Nations.

Vernez, Georges, and Kevin F. McCarthy. 1996. *The Costs of Immigration to Taxpayers: Analytical and Policy Issues*. Santa Monica, Calif.: Rand Corporation.

Wallerstein, Immanuel. 1988. *The Modern-World System III: The Second Era of Great Expansion of the Capitalist World-Economy, 1730–1840s*. New York: Academic Press.

———. 1974. *The Modern World System*. Vol. 1. New York: Academic Press.

Walzer, Michael. 1983. *Spheres of Justice*. New York: Basic Books.

Ward, Kathryn B., ed. 1990. *Women Workers and Global Restructuring*. Ithaca, N.Y.: ILR Press.

Weil, Patrick. 1991. *La France et ses étrangers*. Paris: Calmann-Levy.

Weiner, Myron. 1995. *The Global Migration Crisis*. New York: HarperCollins.

Wiegand, Wolfgang. 1991. "The Reception of American Law in Europe." *American Journal of Comparative Law* 39, no. 2: 229–48..

Williamson, Oliver. 1970. *Corporate Control and Business Behavior*. Englewood Cliffs, N.J.: Prentice-Hall.

Wolf, Eric. 1982. *Europe and the People Without History*. Berkeley: University of California Press.

Woodall, Pam. 1995. "The World Economy: Who's in the Driving Seat?" *The Economist* 337, no. 7935: 5–18, 44.

Young, O. R. 1989. *International Cooperation: Building Regimes for Natural Resources and the Environment*. Ithaca, N.Y.: Cornell University Press.

Zolberg, Aristide R. 1990. "The Roots of U.S. Refugee Policy." In Robert Tucker, Charles B. Keely, and Linda Wrigley, eds. *Immigration and U.S. Foreign Policy*. Boulder, Colo.: Westview.

INDEX

Abbott, Kenneth, 58–59

Aboriginal communities, 38

Accountability, x, xi; capital market and, 28, 42, 47–48, 55; civic demands for, 34, 35; economic citizenship and, xiii, 41; human rights codes and, 28

Accounting, 44, 110n22

Africa, 35, 61, 83, 86; *see also* Organization of African States

Agriculture, 81, 82

Alfonsín, Raúl, 98

Algeria, 66, 87

Aman, Alfred C., Jr., 60, 121n13

American Arbitration Association, 110n21

American Convention on Human Rights, 97

Americanization, 17–22, 111n24

American Revolution, 2, 95

Amsterdam stock market, 47

Anglo-American law, 20, 111n22

Anglo-American law firms, 7, 21, 10–11n22, 111n24

Arab nation, 4

Arbitration, 15–16, 27, 62, 109–10n21, 112n31; Anglo-American lawyers and, 21, 110n22; private nature of, 17; WTO and, 26

Arendt, Hannah, 115n9

Argentina, 53

Arias Sánchez, Oscar, 98

Aristotle, 1

Arrighi, Giovanni, 116n19

Asia: export manufacturing zones in, 9; family-/clan-based economies in, 36; globalized law in, 19; immigration from, 83, 84, 85; political culture of, 35; regional economy of, 89

Asylum, 70–72, 79

Atlantic trade, 83

Austerity policies, 13–14n36

Australia, 16

Australian Trade Practices Commission, 57

Austria, 85, 86

Authorship, 112n30

Bank for International Settlements, 43, 109n19

Bankruptcies, 24

Banks: early 1980s crisis of, 121n12; Eurodollars and, 117n21; government regulation of, 48; international lending by, 12; new financial institutions and, 52, 111–12n27; small investors and, 54; see also Central banks

Belgium, 87, 88

Berlin Wall, 86

Black Wednesday (1992), 51

Bodin, Jean, 1

Bond markets, 43, 45–46, 51, 53

Bond-rating agencies, 16–17, 111n25; see also Credit-rating agencies

Border controls: conflicting dynamics in, 63, 70, 91–92, 93; effectiveness of, 77; sovereignty and, 70

Braudel, Fernand, 116n19

Brazil, 53

Brazilian Conselho Administrativo de Defesa Economica, 57

Bretton Woods system, 49, 58, 117n21; see also General Agreement on Tariffs and Trade

Britain, see United Kingdom

Bush administration, 54

Business firms, *see* Corporations

California, 77, 102–3

Canada, 68

Canadian Bureau of Competition Policy, 57

Capital circulation, 6; distortions of, 54; immigration and, xv, xvi, 92, 93, 120n9; liberalization of, 42; middle-income jobs and, 40; national infrastructure for, 28; public debt and, 49–50; volume of, 44, 45; *see also* Financial markets

Capitalism, 36, 116n19

Carbonneau, Thomas, 111n24

Caribbean Basin countries, 78, 83, 85, 86, 93

Carter, Jimmy, 98

Catholic Church, 4

Central America, 85, 119n7

Central banks, 21–23, 49, 52–53; *see also* Bank for International Settlements

Central Europe, 85

Central Intelligence Agency (U.S.), 123n35

China, 8

Cities: diplomatic negotiation among, 4; financial markets in, 12; global, xii, 12, 109n18; Islamic, 36; Japanese, 89

Citizenship, xi, xii–xiii,xiv; conditions for, 114n4; destabilization of, 36, 114n5, 120–21n9; feudalism and, 114n2; Hague Convention on, 70; history of, 34–36, 114n11; immigrant rights and, 64, 95, 101, 102–3; universalizing of, 61, 115n8; *see also* Civil rights; Economic citizenship; Naturalization

City-leagues, 3

City-states, 3, 35

Civil rights, 34, 72, 102; *see also* Political rights

Clan-based systems, *see* Kinship-based systems

Class inequality, 115n12

Clerical factories, 8

Cold War, 85

Colonialism, 71, 82, 83, 86, 87; *see also* Postcolonialism

Commercial agriculture, 81, 82

Commercial arbitration, *see* Arbitration

Commercial banks, *see* Banks

Commodity chains, 108n14

Commodity futures, 47

Common law, *see* Anglo-American law

Communications technology, xi, 12, 42, 98

Computer networks, xi, 42, 46, 52

Conflict resolution, *see* Arbitration

Contracts, 27, 109n21, 112n31

Convention of The Hague (1930), 70

Convention on Refugee Problems in Africa (1969), 119n3

Convention on Refugees (1952), 70

Convention on the Political Rights of Women (1981), 97

Convention on the Prevention and Punishment of Genocide (1948), 97

Corporate lawyers, 21

Corporate services industry, 6, 11

Corporations, 6; credit-rating processes and, 16–17; denationalization and, 28; derivatives and, 47, 117n26; economic citizenship of, xiv, 41; geographic dispersal of, 7, 9; global cities and, 109n18; headquarter sites of, 11; integration of, 9, 108n14; Japanese hospitality to, 89; legal guarantees and, 15, 112n31; new legal regimes and, 26; overseas affiliates of, 9–10; relative strength of, 26; Russian, 116n14; structured environment of, 113n34; taxation of, 8

Council of Europe, 97

Court of International Commercial Arbitration, 110n21

Courts, *see* Judiciaries

Credit, 48, 52

Credit cards, 49

Credit-rating agencies, 7, 16–17, 27, 112n27; *see also* Bond-rating agencies

Credit Suisse, 19

Currency devaluation, 53

Currency markets: growth of, 43; interest rates and, 49; national debt and, 52; new technologies and, 6, 22; *see also* Capital circulation

Debt, 49–50, 52, 53
Decentered sovereignty, 29–30, 33, 65, 104
Declaration of Independence, 96
Declaration of the Rights of Man and Citizen, 96
Declaration on the Human Rights of Individuals Who Are Not Citizens of the Countries in Which They Live, 123n31
Democracy: capital market and, 54; class inequality and, 115n12; economic well-being and, 40; French Revolution and, 34; international status and, 61, 114n3
Denationalization, xii, 33, 64, 65; in developing countries, 9; factors in, 30; immigration and, xiv
Depression (1929–39), 45
Deregulation, 14, 59; dual roles of, 27; of financial institutions, 52; of financial markets, 13, 42; of interest rates, 48; legal innovations as, 13
Derivatives, 47, 117n26
Devalued currencies, 53
Developed countries, xiv, xvi; citizenship in, 37; clerical operations in, 8; corporate centralization in, 10, 11; economic distress in, xiii, 40; financial markets in, 12; GDP of, 43; immigration to, 67, 68–105; interest rate deregulation in, 48; legal regimes of, 17; Mexican crisis and, 23; reforms demanded by, 25; state participation in, 29, 91; *see also* Organization for Economic Cooperation and Development; Western countries
Developing countries: Americanization and, 20; austerity policies of, 113–14n36; denationalization in, 9; exports of, 81; poverty in, 40; reforms demanded of, 25; state participation in, 29, 93
Dezalay, Yves, 16, 18, 21, 109n21, 110n22

Digitalization, *see*
  Electronic space
Diplomatic rights, 4, 13, 107n8
Disadvantaged populations,
  62, 72
Disintermediation, 111n27
Dominican Republic, 78, 79, 85
Dutch East Indies Company,
  108n11

Earnings, xiii, 28, 39
Eastern Europe, 61, 83
East Germany, 86
Economic citizenship, xiii, xiv,
  33–62, 115n11
Electoral politics, 35, 47, 55, 66;
  see also Political rights
Electronic cash, 52
Electronic space, 21–22, 46,
  108n18; *see also* Computer
  networks; Telecommuni-
  cations
El Salvador, 78, 82, 85, 119–20n7
Employment, *see* Labor
England, *see* United Kingdom
Environmental issues, 25, 60
Equities markets, *see*
  Stock markets
hnicity, 82, 120–21n9
ic lobbies, 72, 74, 76, 84

Eurodollars, 117n21
Euronotation (firm), 111n25
Europe: asylum policies in, 79;
  bond-rating agencies in, 16;
  citizenship in, 35, 36, 37; ethnicity in, 120–21n9; ethnic
  lobbies in, 66; French legal
  services for, 110n22; globalized law in, 19; human rights
  regime in, 98; immigration
  from, 77, 86; immigration to,
  86, 87; migration within, 79;
  monetary system of,
  116–17n19; neoliberal economics and, 18; securitization
  in, 47; stock market deregulation in, 13; traditional law
  in, 20, 22; *see also* Central
  Europe; Eastern Europe;
  Medieval Europe; Northern
  Europe; Western Europe
European Commission, 57
European Community, 21, 37,
  61, 79, 92–93; *see also*
  European Union
European Convention on
  Human Rights (1950), 97,
  98–99, 122n25
European Court of Human
  Rights, 99, 122n25

European Economic Union, 33

European Exchange Rate Mechanism, 52

European Union, 30; immigration issue and, xv, 70, 74, 92; Mediterranean countries and, 79; voting rights in, 102; *see also* European Community

Exchange rates, *see* Currency markets

Exclusive territoriality, xii, 1, 3, 34, 65

Export-oriented agriculture, 82

Export-oriented manufacturing, 81, 84

Export processing zones, 8–9

Extraterritoriality, 4, 13, 108n10

Exxon Corporation, 10

Factories, 8

Family-based systems, 3, 36, 82

Family reunification, 72, 77

Feudalism, 114n2; *see also* Medieval Europe

Financial industry, 6, 89

Financial institutions, *see* Banks; Savings-and-loan associations

Financial markets, 7, 12–13, 41–47; accountability and, 28, 42, 47–48, 55; Americanization of, 19; digitalization of, 22, 46; dominance of, 27, 40, 62; economic citizenship and, xiv, 41; Mexican crisis and, 23, 24; potential growth of, 115–16n17; precursors of, 116–17n19; regulation of, 108–9n18, 111–12n27, 117n21; state and, 47–55, 59, 70; *see also* Bond markets; Currency markets; Investors; Stock markets

Financial Times, 19–20

Finnish immigrants, 87

Firms, *see* Corporations

Ford Motor Company, 10, 108n18

Foreign aid, 78

Foreign exchange, *see* Currency markets

Foreign Relations Authorization Act (1977), 73

Fortune 500 firms, 49

France: Algerians in, 67, 87; bank loans by, 13; European Convention on Human Rights and, 99; family re-

France (*continued*)
    fication issue and, 72; immigration to, 68, 71, 87; legal practice in, 22, 110–11n22; private debt in, 52
Franchising, 20
Franck, Thomas, 61, 114n3
Fraud, 117n24
Freedom, 115n9; *see also* Democracy
Free trade, 25
Free trade zones, 9, 30
French Antilles, 87
French Conseil de la Concurrence, 57
French Guyana, 87
French Revolution, 2, 34, 95
Futures, 47

Garth, Bryant, 16, 18, 21, 109n21, 110n22
General Agreement on Tariffs and Trade: Americanization and, 20; on border controls, 70; "private"/"public" dichotomy in, 58–59; service workers and, xv, 7, 93; Tokyo Round, 118n31; Uruguay Round, 7, 59, 118n31, 118n32; WTO and, 25–26

General Motors Corporation, 10
Genoa, 116–17n19
German Democratic Republic, 86
German Federal Cartel Office, 57
Germany: asylum in, 70, 79; bank loans by, 13; city-leagues in, 3; currency of, 54; family reunification issue and, 72; human rights regime in, 64, 99; immigration to, 68, 69, 85, 86, 88; overseas affiliates of, 10; private debt in, 52
Gillette/Wilkinson merger, 57
Goldman Sachs Securities (firm), 24
Gold standard, 45, 46
Governance, xi, xii; private mechanisms for, 16, 27, 61; state participation in, 23; transformation of, 57; *see also* Regulatory regimes
Great Depression, 45
Greece, 34, 86
Grotius, Hugo, 5, 108n11

Hague Convention (1930), 70
Haiti, 85, 120n7
Hanseatic League, 3

Hedge funds, 54

Helsinki Accords (1975), 73

Hintze, Otto, 114*n*2

Hobbes, Thomas, 1

Homeowners, 24

Housing construction, 48

Human rights: accountability and, 28; asylum and, 70; citizenship and, 38, 115*n*8; federal citations of, 122*n*26; immigration and, xv, 64, 71, 77, 99–103, 119–20*nn*7, 8; international conventions on, 96–97; lawful expulsions and, 119*n*5; sovereignty and, 30, 34, 64, 94–104

IBCA (firm), 111*n*25

Identity, 38, 121*n*9

Illegal aliens, *see* Undocumented immigrants

Immigration, xiv–xvii, 7, 63–105, 119–120*n*7, 120*n*8, 120–21*n*9; in EC, 37, 92; policy formulation for, 32; *see also* Asylum; Refugees; Return migration; Undocumented immigrants

Immigration Act (1965), 77

Immigration and Naturalization Service (U.S.), 73, 75

Immigration Reform and Control Act (1986), 72, 80, 121*n*12

India, 78, 86, 115–16*n*17

Indochina, 78, 119*n*2

Industrial engineering services, 110*n*22

Industrialization, 36; *see also* Manufacturing

Industrialized countries, *see* Developed countries

Inflation, 53

Information services, 6, 110*n*22; *see also* Credit-rating agencies

Information technology, *see* Electronic space

Institutional investors, 46, 54, 116*n*18; *see also* Pension funds

Insurance companies, 46

Inter-American Commission on Human Rights, 97

Interest groups, 103–4; *see also* Ethnic lobbies

Interest rates, 48–49, 51, 117–18*n*26

Intermediation, 111n27; *see also* Mediation

International Bank for Reconstruction and Development, 20

International Business Machines Corporation, 8, 10

International Chamber of Commerce, 110n21

International Convention on the Elimination of All Forms of Racial Discrimination (1965), 97

International Convention on the Protection of the Rights of All Migrant Workers and Members of Their Families (1990), 72, 100, 123n30

International Court of Justice, 122n25

International Covenant on Civil and Political Rights (1976), 96–97

International Covenant on Economic, Social, and Cultural Rights (1976), 96–97

ternational Labour Organization, 100–101

International Monetary Fund, 20, 51, 121n12

Investments, 40, 82, 84, 116n18

Investors: capital available to, 44; as democratic exemplar, 53, 54; Mexican crisis and, 23, 50–51; mobility of, 42; new exchanges for, 115–16n17; *see also* Financial markets; Institutional investors

Iraq, 43

Ireland, 86, 88

Irish Fair Trade Commission, 57

Islamic societies, 35, 36

Israel, 80

Italy, 3, 79, 87, 88

Jackson, John, 58

Jacobson, David, 122n26

Jamaica, 85

Japan: bank loans by, 13; bond-rating agencies in, 16; border controls in, 63; currency of, 54; ethnic lobbies in, 66; family-/clan-based economy of, 36; globalized law in, 19; immigration to, 71, 73, 88, 89, 94, 120n8; naturalization policy of, 68, 69; overseas plants of, 8; private debt in, 52

Judiciaries, xvi; accountability through, 35; arbitration and, 109–10n21; corporate transactions and, 21–22; immigrant rights and, 72, 99–100, 102, 119–20n7; Universal Declaration and, 122n26

Kalberg, Stephen, 114n4

Kennedy, Duncan, 118n30

Keynes, John Maynard, 45

Kinship-based systems, 3, 36, 82

Labor: employer power over, 118n30; migrant, 72, 81, 87–90, 119n5, 120n8; recruitment of, 82, 83, 87; in service sector, xv–xvi, 7, 93; of undocumented aliens, 89, 90, 100, 120n8; see also Earnings; Unemployment

Latin America, 9, 35

Law firms: Anglo-American, 7, 21, 110n22, 111n24; French, 22, 110–11n22; multinational, 26, 110–11n22

League of Nations, 3

Legal concepts, 112n30

Legalism, 58

Legal system: globalization of, 17–19; hierarchy within, 101, 102; human rights and, 95, 96; implementation of, 113–14n36; implicit permissions in, 56; national regulation and, 59–60; new governance systems and, 27, 61; privatization of, 56; rights guaranteed by, 27; Shapiro on, 113n35; sovereignty and, 2, 70; see also Anglo-American law; Judiciaries; Private legal regimes

Legitimacy zone, 55–56

Lex mercatoria, 105n24

London Court of International Commercial Arbitration, 110n21

Luxembourg, 13

McKinsey Global Institute, 44, 115n17

Manhattan, 30; see also New York City

Manufacturing, 24, 81–82, 84; see also Offshore production

Maquiladoras, 8
Mare Liberum doctrine, 5
Marginal populations, 62, 72
Maritime trade routes, 108*n*11
Marshall, T. H., 39, 115*n*12
Mattingly, Garrett, 4, 107*n*8
Mediation, 109*n*21; *see also*
    Intermediation
Medieval Europe: citizenship in,
    34; international financial
    market of, 116*n*19; res pub-
    lica christiana of, 55; right of
    embassy in, 4, 13, 107*n*8;
    transition from, 3; *see also*
    Feudalism
Mediterranean countries, 79,
    83, 87
Mergers, 57
Mexico, 8, 23–24, 50–51, 53, 80
Middle Ages, *see* Medieval
    Europe
Middle class, 40
Migrant labor, 72, 81, 87–90,
    119*n*5, 120*n*8
Military actions, 82
Military aid, 78
Minority rights, 3
Moody's Investors Service, 16,
    45–46
Moroccans, 87

Mortgages, 48
Moynihan-Frank Amendment
    (1987), 73
Multilateralism, 112*n*32
Multilateral Trade Negotiations,
    118*n*31
Multiperspectival institutions,
    112*n*32
Muslim societies, 35, 36

Napoleonic Code, 110–11*n*22
National debt, 49, 51, 53
National identity, 121*n*9
Nationally Recognized
    Statistical Rating
    Organizations, 19
National security, 123*n*35
National territoriality, *see*
    Territoriality
Naturalization, 68, 102
Neocolonialism, 82, 86–87; *see
    also* Postcolonialism
Neoliberal economics, 18, 25
Netherlands, 87, 99, 102,
    116*n*19; *see also* Amsterdam
    stock market
New York City, 113*n*34; *see also*
    Manhattan
New York Convention (1958),
    110*n*21

Nomadic societies, 3

Non-governmental organizations, 104, 105; *see also* Supranational institutions

North America, 13, 19, 36, 63, 73

North American Free Trade Agreement, xvi, 7, 70, 93

Northern Europe, 3

Northern Industrialization Program (Mexico), 8

Ocean trade routes, 108*n*11

Offshore production, 7–8, 82

Orange County (Calif.), 49

Organization for Economic Cooperation and Development, 44, 49

Organization of African States, 119*n*3

Organization of American States, 97

Pakistan, 78

Pax Britannica, 45, 55

Pension funds, 44, 46, 54; *see also* Retirement benefits

Personal identity, 38

Philippines, 78, 82, 85

Plants (factories), 8

Polanyi, Karl, 117*n*19

Political electorate, *see* Electoral politics

Political rhetoric, 66, 67

Political rights, 61, 72, 77; *see also* Voting rights

Popular culture, 20

Popular sovereignty, 2, 101; *see also* Democracy

Portugal, 79, 87, 108*n*11

Postcolonialism, 61; *see also* Neocolonialism

Poverty, 39–40, 68, 81, 85

Pragmatism, 58

Private corporations, *see* Corporations

Private debt, 52

Private legal regimes, 3; Americanization of, 20, 21; denationalization and, 29–30, 65; dual agenda of, 27; rise of, 5, 13–16, 54, 112*n*31; sovereignty and, 31, 33–34; state institutions and, 26, 28

Privatization, 25, 59; *see also* Denationalization; Deregulation

Professional persons, 94

Property rights, 27, 112*n*30, 118*n*30

Proposition 187 (Calif.), 102–3
Protocol to the Covenant on Civil and Political Rights (1976), 97
Public debt, 49–50, 51, 54
Public services, 76,101

Quantum Fund, 51
Quasi-governmental institutions, xv, 104

Rating agencies, *see* Credit-rating agencies
Reagan administration, 49, 51, 54
Recruitment, 82, 83, 87
Refugee Act (1980), 73
Refugees: border controls and, 63, 91–92, 93; citizenship issue and, 38; foreign aid and, 78; human rights of, 64; regimes for, 68, 70, 119n2; from socialist bloc, 75; statistics on, 67, 85; U.S. courts and, 99
Regulation Q, 48
Regulatory regimes: competition in, 19; global cities and, 108n18; offshoring and, 9; private, 15–17; state, 29,

47–55, 59–60, 111–12n27, 117n21; *see also* Border controls; Deregulation
Renationalization, xiv, 63, 64, 66
Res publica, 55
Retirement benefits, 102; *see also* Pension funds
Return migration, 68, 80
Rights, xii; of asylum, 70; of economic citizenship, 40–41, 55, 56; of embassy, 4, 13, 107n8; of minorities, 3; of refugees, 70; of resident immigrants, 72; in welfare state, xiii, 39; *see also* Civil rights; Human rights; Political rights; Property rights; Social rights
Robertson, R., 113n34
Roepke, Wilhelm, 55
Roman Catholic Church, 4
Roosevelt, Franklin D., 75
Rosenau, J. N., 17
Rubin, Robert, 24
Ruggie, John, 26, 112n32
Russian stock market, 115–16n17

Salacuse, Jeswald, 110n22
Salvador, 78, 82, 85, 119–20n7
Sanctuary movement, 119n7

Savings, 116n18

Savings-and-loan associations, 48, 117n24

Schuck, Peter H., 102

Securities and Exchange Commission (U.S.), 19

Securities markets, *see* Stock markets

Securitization, 46–47

Security issues, 123n35

Self-determination, 61, 101, 103

Service workers, xv–xvi, 7, 93–94

Shapiro, Martin, 18–19, 20, 113n35

Sinclair, Timothy J., 16–17, 111n26

Singapore, 36

Slavery, 83

Small businesses, 24

Social class, 115n12

Social fund, 49, 51, 54

Social interest groups, *see* Interest groups

Socialist bloc, 61, 75, 85

Social rights, 39, 40, 72, 77

Social services, 76, 101

"Soft security" issues, 123n35

Soros, George, 51

South Asia, 84

Southeast Asia, 35, 84

South Korea, 36, 85

Soviet Union, 61, 80; *see also* Russian stock market

Spain, 79, 87, 99, 108n11

Special interests, *see* Interest groups

Speculators, 45

Standard and Poor's Ratings Group, 16

Stateless people, *see* Asylum; Refugees

Stock markets, 13, 43–44; *see also* Amsterdam stock market; Russian stock market

Sugar, 78

Supranational institutions, xvi, 3; immigration policy and, 105; sovereignty and, 30, 31, 33, 65; *see also* Non-governmental organizations

Sweden, 68, 87, 102

Swiss Bank Corporation, 19

Switzerland, 13, 22, 68, 87, 88

Tahiti, 87

Taiwan, 36

Taxation, 9, 77

Telecommunications, xi, xii, 12, 42, 98

Tenth Amendment, 121n13

Territoriality: economic globalization and, 5, 7–13, 31; exclusive, xii, xiii, 1, 3, 34, 65; *see also* enationalization; Renationalization

Thailand, 120n8

Tokyo Round, 118n31

Trial lawyers, 21

Tunisians, 87

Turkey, 99

Turkish immigrants, 86, 87, 88

Undeveloped countries, *see* Developing countries

Undocumented immigrants, 67, 85; international covenants on, 100, 123nn30, 31; in Japan, 89, 90, 120n8; rights-sovereignty tension and, 64, 95; in U.S., 99–100, 102

Unemployment, xiii, 39, 40; in Caribbean Basin, 78–79; credit rating and, 111n26; immigration and, 81, 85

Unionized labor, 81–82

United Kingdom: bank loans by, 3; currency of, 52; EC legal business and, 20–21; immigration to, 83, 86; neoliberal economics and, 18; *see also* Anglo-American law; Pax Britannica

United Nations: human rights violations and, 99; on refugees, 73; Universal Declaration of Human Rights, 2, 96, 122n26; U.S. dues to, 31

United Nations Centre for Transnational Corporations, 108n13

United Nations Charter, 2

United Nations Commission on International Trade Law, 110n21

United Nations Conference on Trade and Development, 108n13

United Nations Demographic Yearbook, 84

United Nations General Assembly, 72, 100, 123n31

United Nations High Commissioner for Refugees, 120n7

United Nations Human Rights Committee, 97

United States: banking in, 12, 117n21; bond-rating agencies of, 16–17; borrowing by, 49, 51, 54; capital/immigrant regimes in, 92; capital markets of, 45; currency of, 53–54; developing countries and, 24; ethnicity in, 120–21n9; ethnic lobbies in, 66, 74, 76; former socialist bloc and, 61; GATT support in, 26; human rights regime in, 64, 96, 99; immigration to, 68, 71, 75–79, 83, 84; intergovernmental relations in, 76, 118n13; Japanese plants in, 8; legal regime in, 113n35, 118n30; litigation in, 109n21; Mexican crisis and, 23, 50; military actions of, 82; neoliberal economics and, 18; new financial institutions in, 51–52; noncitizenshiplike features of, 37; overseas affiliates of, 9–10; private debt in, 52; refugee policy of, 119n2; sanctuary movement in, 119n7; savings-and-loan crisis in, 48; securitization in, 47; social services in, 102; "soft security" issues in, 123n35; undocumented aliens in, 89, 99–102; UN dues of, 31; see also Americanization; Anglo-American law

United States Central Intelligence Agency, 123n35

United States Congress, 23, 51, 75, 76, 121n12

United States Constitution, 73, 96; see also Tenth Amendment

United States Declaration of Independence, 96

United States Department of Defense, 123n35

United States Department of Justice, 57, 75

United States Department of Labor, 75

United States Department of State, 24, 123n35

United States Federal Reserve System, 53

United States Immigration and Naturalization Service, 73, 75

United States Securities and Exchange Commission, 19

United States Treasury, 24

United States Treasury bonds, 43

Universal Declaration of Human Rights, 2, 96, 97, 122n26

Urban Institute, 77

Uruguay Round, 7, 59, 118nn31, 32

Value-added chains, 108n14

Vertical integration, 108n14

Virtualization, *see* Electronic space

Voting rights, 42, 102

Weber, Max, 35

Welfare state, xiii, 39, 40, 115n12

Western countries: citizenship concept of, 34–35, 36, 37; economic concepts of, 18; human capital from, 94; immigration to, 85–86; legal concepts of, 112n30; social-political theory of, xii, 37

Western Europe: border controls in, 63; human rights regime in, 96; immigration to, 73, 83, 89; monarchies in, 3; social services in, 102

Western Hemisphere, 93; *see also* Latin America; North America

West Germany, 86

Wilkinson/Gillette merger, 57

World Population Prospects, 84

World Trade Organization, 7, 25–26, 30, 59, 118n31

World War II, 75

Yugoslavia, 104

Yugoslav immigrants, 67, 86, 87

Designer: María Giuliani
Text: Fournier
Compositor: Columbia University Press
Printer: Edwards Brothers
Binder: Edwards Brothers